CREATING TIME

VICKIE GRAY

ISBN: 1466333529
ISBN 13: 9781466333529

Creating Time

by Vickie Gray

Dedication

For Paul

Contents

Acknowledgements i

Introduction v

Part 1: Go Beyond Keeping Promises: The Simple Rules

—The Core Commitments 1

Part 2: Keep A Toolbox: The Simple Tools

—The Core Protocols 13

Chapter 1: Use All The Resources You've Got: Ask For Help 15

Chapter 2: Be A No-Feedback Zone: Investigate 29

Chapter 3: Share Mad, Sad, Glad, and Afraid: Check In 41

Chapter 4: Claim Your Freedom To Leave: Check Out 53

Chapter 5: Know And Get What You Want: Personal Alignment 61

Chapter 6: Check Intent Early and Often: Intention Check 75

Chapter 7: Get Unanimous Decisions: Decider and Resolution 85

Chapter 8: Give and Get Only Value: Perfection Game 99

Chapter 9: Light A Fire: Scary Idea 109

Chapter 10: Go First: Protocol Check 119

Chapter 11: Be A Great Boss 127

Chapter 12: Take It Home 137

Afterword 143

Notes From Human Systems Dynamics 149

Bibliography 161

Biography of the Author 164

Acknowledgements

Jim and Michele McCarthy's leadership, wisdom, mentorship, and caring friendship have been threads of inspiration that supported me through learning about teams, organizations, and myself for the past eleven years. One day I'll ask them for enough help.

The participants and instructors of the McCarthy BootCamps have been my learning partners, giving me a chance to practice, practice, and practice the Core Protocols and Core Commitments. They are my extended team, helping me achieve my goals while we all work toward a world where we all have the time we want.

My coaching and consulting clients have given me a chance to do field research in the application of the simple rules and tools in "the wild," particularly in the complex environment of technology operations where there is little certainty or agreement about the future, the speed of change is dizzying, and the time-eating monster lurks around every corner. They have been inspiring and courageous partners in my learning about the astonishing results that can be achieved by a rigorous discipline of simplicity on teams, and the painful consequences of the alternative.

Dr. Glenda Eoyang, Wendy Morris, Dr. Kevin Kreitman, and the Human Systems Dynamics Associates Network are wise mentors in my quest to understand the science of the simple rules and tools. For many years I knew the tools worked, but I didn't know why. My introduction to Dr. Eoyang's work on complexity in human systems, particularly her three-variable CDE model, has given me the scientific basis I had been seeking. My long-term vision is to bring the Core System and Human Systems Dynamics together. The first step toward that vision is this book.

A few brave people volunteered to read and review early drafts of this book. For the insights, ideas, and wisdom they brought me, I am deeply grateful: Paul Reeves, Michele McCarthy, Jim McCarthy, Yves Hanoulle, Catherine Gray, Michael Josefowicz, David Sanders, Eric Mignot, Susan Bone, Jennifer Sertl, Bernard Notarianni, Deanne Oikle, and Craig McQueen.

My partner, Paul—Core BootCamp Instructor, editor, coach, master coffeemaker, cheerer-upper, and brilliant team whisperer—gets all the other kudos. I suppose there might be an alternative universe in which I was able to get to this point in my life without his cheerful wisdom, his calm abiding, his lighthearted perseverance, and his unconditional love and kindness, but it must be a grim and sorry place indeed.

Introduction

What would you do with more time?

Play with your kids more?

Volunteer?

Go hiking in Patagonia?

Take a nap?

Fix what's wrong with the world?

Time is the most precious resource we don't have enough of. How often in the past week did you say something like the following?:

- "I didn't get to it because I was so swamped."
- "There just wasn't enough time."
- "There are only twenty-four hours in the day and only one of me."

Once time is gone, it's gone. Spent. Like money. Can't get it back. And every moment you spend in meetings listening to people tell you what they don't like about the team they're on, or the work they're doing, every hour second-guessing your idea, and every sleepless minute wondering about someone's intent is another lost moment.

The time you spend is never coming back. Most of us believe there's nothing we can do about time. To most of us, it's fixed, finite, and out of our control. And that's true if that's what we believe.

What we believe about time changes time itself. When we believe we can't change time and we'll never have enough of it, we bring into being a monstrous entity.

This monster has a soft, reasonable voice. It might sound like the nice, hardworking people who are too busy to take lunch. Or like the boss who rewards you for staying late and arriving early. It says we have to stay silent when we have a better idea, or have our voice heard when we have nothing new to say. It sounds rational and trustworthy. It sounds familiar.

It seeks out meetings, committees, complex process, and politics. Fence-sitting, politeness, conflict without resolution, and drama feed it. It loves people who multitask, double-book meetings, communicate complicated ideas by email, and try to do everything without help. It tells us people will be impressed when we say we don't have time, when we're too busy to make it to a social event or even to take care of ourselves. In comfortable tones it assures us that we've accomplished something others will admire, so we can feel safe in the knowledge we're valuable.

Have you ever worked for a company that gives out spot awards to people for never missing a day of work? Or for always being at their desk before everyone else? Or for working through the weekend to fix a problem? The monster breeds there. Try this experiment: cancel all your meetings next week. Feel that resistance in yourself? Hear the voice in your head saying, "I can't do that!"? You just helped the creature's offspring slither into reality.

It doesn't want us to know that time is in our control. Even more dangerous to it is the fact that we can create time ourselves. And when we control and create time the monster ceases to exist.

A few people know how to control and create time. They are the ones having fun, enjoying their teammates, creating great things, and delivering them when they promised. They take long weekends, leave work early, and still deliver more than anyone else. They play with their families, communities, and friends, and they change the world.

Have you ever had that pit-of-the-stomach dread as you sit in a meeting, and you look at the clock and realize two hours of your life has gone by that you can't get back? Ever. Add to that the hours commuting to get here for the meeting. You look around the table and realize everyone else is anaesthetized, compliant. You rage inside but continue to sit and participate, locked in the belief there's nothing you can do. Every time someone in the room thinks there's a better way and says nothing, the stronger the monster gets.

But the first time someone in that meeting states the truth, shares an idea, or asks for action, it begins to lose power. Try it. Make a decision. Suggest ending the meeting, leave yourself if necessary, and immediately create a prototype. Share your best idea and ask for others to improve it. Feel that dread replaced by the thrill of freedom? Because you did something different, the monster has begun to lose its grip on you.

Imagine if you weren't alone in making these choices. If you were on a team that can create time it would feel like this: Energy is high. You're fired up about the work you're doing and so are all the other team members. You seek them out on a daily basis to get their ideas on the work you're doing. You admire them and respect their skills and abilities, but more importantly, you trust them and enjoy their company. When conflict comes up, you start the resolution from a place of respect and curiosity.

You find the work fascinating and know that this team will turn the original good idea into something exceptional. You have fun together and help each other, and the work just flows. What would take another team weeks to do, this team delivers in hours. Any of you can leave and look after personal business and trust the team to deliver. Time for sharing new ideas, helping each other with other projects, or taking a nap is always available because time passes in a kind of slow motion. Minutes seem to appear out of nowhere. These teams create time. They live in a monster-free world.

Most teams, however, can barely keep a grip on the seconds slipping by. If you were on one of the monster's favorite teams, it would look like this: Every interaction is like rowing through heavy seas, burdened with stacks of unspoken minor irritations and barely contained cynicism. Unresolved conflict eats up time and energy like rust. "I didn't get it done—I was just swamped," is the mutually acceptable explanation for a broken promise. You spend your day in one of two places: in front of a computer or in meetings. The few people you actually speak to complain that there isn't enough staff and too much to do in the time available. On these teams the power of the creature is almost limitless.

Most of us have seen both the miracle and the torture of working on teams or in groups. We might have seen or been on a great team that creates time, and thought it was a fluke. Almost everyone believes that those teams are somehow created, managed, and controlled by a smart and educated outside force, a facilitator, leader, or project manager who identifies roles and responsibilities, mediates conflicts, and assigns tasks.

But great teams don't need heroes to ride into town and fix what's wrong. That's not because the products they're creating are easier to create. It's not how their workplace is laid out, what kind of project methodology they use, or whether they are face-to-face or virtual.

It's because they believe they can control time, and they have access to a toolbox for creating more of it. This book is about the tools in that toolbox.

How Those Tools Came To Be

If you were curious about tools to create time, you might develop a theory about what people do to save time. Then you'd test that theory. It could take years and waste a lot of time before you had proof it worked every time. Many of the principles used in Western workplaces in the last two hundred years have used this approach.

An alternative is to find people who already excel at what you want to do, and simply do exactly what they do. So if you were going to learn what great teams do to create time, you would watch great teams and find out specifically, moment by moment, what they're doing. Then, of course, you'd want to be sure this wasn't a fluke. So you'd find another great team creating time. And another.

You'd want to watch enough teams to see what was universally successful. One or two teams wouldn't be enough to see the common patterns regardless of culture, status, or language. You'd need lots, hundreds of them. You'd study what they do, write it down, try it out on other teams, test it, and then do that again. Once you figured out what really makes these teams tick, the secret sauce, and could reproduce the results on any team anywhere, then you might have confidence that you had a reliable set of tools anyone could use.

If someone else had already done all these steps, that would be even better. You'd already be taking control of time.

Someone else has.

Jim and Michele McCarthy founded a team laboratory in 1996. For fifteen years, Jim and Michele scientifically studied and codified team behaviors, good and bad, successful and unsuccessful. They tested their findings on subsequent teams, recorded the results, tested again on the next teams, and on and on, in a continually iterated experiment called BootCamp. Their commitment to rigor, completeness, and repeatability in testing these tools is legendary. Jim and Michele's book about their findings, *Software For Your Head*, was a groundbreaking study of patterns and antipatterns on teams, densely packed with detailed observations of what works and what doesn't when people collaborate on a shared idea. The most exciting outcome of the team laboratory was the highly polished and tested tools called the Core Commitments and Core Protocols.

This book is a way of bringing the Core Commitments and Core Protocols to people who believe they just don't have time to read something as rich and deep as Software For Your Head. Think of this book as The Core System 101. It's also a way of showing that time really is in our control if we have the right tools in our toolbox.

The monster, by the way, is very worried that I've brought up the possibility that what you need to create time already exists, you don't have to start from scratch to do all this work yourself, and you can simply start using the tools to create time at will. It's hoping you'll pay no attention.

WHAT'S IN THIS BOOK

This book is the user's guide to the time-creation toolbox. The toolbox contains two basic sets of tools: The Core Commitments and the Core Protocols. If the Core Commitments and Core Protocols are adopted by a team that understands and uses them consistently, the monster starves.

In each chapter I will do the following:

- Give an example of how I've seen the monster appear in a business, family, or community.
- Illustrate how great teams create time.
- Give you the time-creation tool in its entirety.
- Offer an example of how you and I can use it to create time for ourselves.

Most teams, families, and communities are together to create something. For the sake of brevity, when I talk about what a team produces, I will use the catchall word "product."

Though this book focuses on using the toolbox at work, great teams eventually try the tools everywhere else. So, at the end of the book I also offer some ideas for taking the tools home.

For those of us who want to explore the reasons the tools work, the emerging models from the discipline of Human Systems Dynamics and the work of Dr. Glenda Eoyang offer an elegant model for organizing our thinking about human systems such as teams. I have included a brief outline of my own early thinking about the subject at the end of the book.

The Core Protocols and Core Commitments are a living, evolving set of rules and tools in the public domain. So while I have included the most current version of the protocols at the time of publishing, I encourage you to download the latest set of Core Commitments and Core Protocols for free from www.liveingreatness.com.

Finally, like any tool, becoming comfortable with these tools takes patience, practice and support. If they feel uncomfortable at first, you're not alone. Like ice skating, playing piano or learning to speak a new language, it's the practice that makes the difference.

I look forward to finding out what you do with the time you create.

Vickie Gray

Part 1:

Go Beyond Keeping Promises

The Simple Rules—The Core Commitments

"Hold yourself responsible for a higher standard than anybody expects of you. Never excuse yourself."

Henry Ward Beecher

Feeding the Monster

The new intern is sitting in his cubicle. No one is quite sure what he's doing. The chip bags and empty cans are piling up around his computer, and he's sitting with his feet up on the desk, texting on his phone.

The monster waits for the phrases, "It's not fair," and "Why does he get away with that?" It can hear that kind of conversation from a mile away. Revenge, retaliation, gossip, complaining, scapegoating, shunning, angry email writing, and emotionally rehashing the situation over dinner with spouses and kids are all exceptionally tasty to the monster.

When we don't have a simple set of rules we can all work within, we each bring our own personal preferences to our judgment of each other's behavior, with time-wasting consequences for them and us.

Do these strategies for "behavior problems" sound familiar? We ignore it, hope it goes away, use performance management to document it after the fact, avoid the person, make the poor performer embarrassed in public, complain about it behind the person's back, work around it, do the work ourselves, hope they get the message, exclude them from team communications, leave the job, leave the company, and let our anger come out with partners, children, and dogs.

Every single conflict-resolution training or book ever written tells us to address the person directly. You've read the books, taken the training. Do you do it? Every time? If you do, you're a member of a rare crowd.

Even if we do address the person who can change the behavior or put us straight about our own, most of the time we just can't call on a prior set of commitments that have been broken. If the offender says, "Everyone does it," we can get angry with her for being bullheaded, but we can't argue she's wrong. Everyone does do it at some point.

What's missing is an agreement on norms or commitments that guide our interactions before we start working together. Sure, we might have those lists up on the walls of our meeting rooms that remind us of rules we learned in kindergarten, like, "Only one person talking at once."

But those aren't the things we really need rules for. Talking over each other starts with thinking over each other. Thinking over each other starts with who we are as a team, how we see each other, and our individual contributions, influence, value, and results. It starts with the questions of where is power, how is it distributed, and who decides when it changes hands? It starts with "Who am I?" and "Who are you?" and "How should we work together?" Those are the kinds of things we need rules for.

And so, in the absence of a clear set of rules, it all gets very messy and complicated. Our motives are complex, and tied up with perception, preferences, biases, expectations, assumptions, and inferences.

Sometimes mediation, conflict-resolution training, group facilitation sessions, or process frameworks can help sort out perceptions and build comprehension. We may come out of facilitated sessions feeling closer and more tolerant of each other. For a time.

But the kinds of conflicts I'm talking about are systemic. And most people just don't have access to the skillful resources required to handle them well on an ongoing basis. So we end up back at work, in the same system again, with the same festering resentment, grudges, drama, avoidance, and other behaviors. And the time-eating monster loves every minute it's in control.

So a clear set of common rules for how we do the basic things people do when they work together is the first tool we want to put in the time-creation toolbox.

But what rules? The organization has simple rules already. Every organization does. They lie under the surface and are the real drivers of the patterns of behavior across teams. Things like, "We hire only smart people." Or "When we have a discussion, everyone has to find a risk inherent in the idea proposed so we don't get surprised in the future." So are those the simple rules we should use? Maybe. In most organizations there are simple rules in play that are adaptive, helpful, and useful.

Sometimes the existing rules have arisen out of a specific event or crisis. For instance, five years ago the former CEO received a call from a key customer complaining his account manager had not replied to him in a timely manner. The CEO announced a rule that requires everyone to reply to any email within twenty-four hours. That rule remains in place today. Is it useful? Was it ever useful?

A more useful rule is one that is more universal. It could define individual accountability in communication against the vision of a delighted customer. An open, high-dimension rule like that can be applied across all forms of communication and achieves the underlying goal of the former, and we hope, current CEO, which is the satisfaction of the customer.

Another organization may have a project-management organization in charge of administering a complex set of processes and procedures. The framework of the processes has grown over a period of years, like ivy on a building, with detailed rules about reporting time, task management, documentation, and meeting agendas. Rules that complicated eventually seem to become not a means to an end but an end in themselves. But a more useful set of rules may simply support the development of products quickly with the maximum transparency and minimum waste.

Can we create our own commonly agreed rules from scratch? Well, we have a hard enough time trying to figure out where to go for lunch without having to agree on commitments for the team. Of course some organizations have an implicit rule called, "Not Invented Here," and they would insist on starting from scratch regardless of how universal and useful a set of tools was from somewhere else. The time-eating monster thrives in companies with the "Not Invented Here" rule.

As we said in the Introduction, a good place to start would be a set of rules that work for most people in most circumstances in most cultures. Fortunately, the Core Commitments fit the bill.

How Great Teams Create Time

The Core Commitments emerged in the laboratory as the teams struggled again and again with all the same time challenges you and I and everyone else face with any group. When these teams discovered rules that created time and blocked the monster, they wrote them down. Every team was offered the rules discovered by the previous teams. There was no obligation to use them, and they had the opportunity to test the rules in whatever way they chose. The rules and tools that worked every time for every team are now the only ones left.

Do people in cultures other than North America accept these rules? Yes. They apply in different cultures, languages, ages, religions, genders, socioeconomic statuses, castes, education levels, and mixed teams of all of the above. All the usual suspects have found these rules create the highest quality time that's monster-proof when used consistently.

Commitment implies an expectation of honor to the promise. If my team and I choose to work with these rules, I have a responsibility to hold myself and the others accountable to them. No one made us do it. There is no parent we can whine at and say, "It isn't fair," and no evil despot we feel the need to sabotage or work around at every opportunity. It's our choice, freely made. The freedom to choose without being controlled, manipulated, or compelled is the toolbox in which we place our time-creation tools.

THE CORE COMMITMENTS

1. I commit to engage when present.
   - ☐ To know and disclose
     - i. what I want,
     - ii. what I think, and
     - iii. what I feel.
   - To always seek effective help.
   - To decline to offer and refuse to accept incoherent emotional transmissions.
   - When I have or hear a better idea than the currently prevailing idea, I will immediately either
     - i. propose it for decisive acceptance or rejection, and/or
     - ii. explicitly seek its improvement.
   - I will personally support the best idea
     - i. regardless of its source,
     - ii. however much I hope an even better idea may later arise, and
     - iii. when I have no superior alternative idea.
2. I will seek to perceive more than I seek to be perceived.
3. I will use teams, especially when undertaking difficult tasks.

4. I will speak always and only when I believe it will improve the general results/effort ratio.
5. I will offer and accept only rational, results-oriented behavior and communication.
6. I will disengage from less productive situations
   - When I cannot keep these commitments,
   - When it is more important that I engage elsewhere.
7. I will do now what must be done eventually and can effectively be done now.
8. I will seek to move forward toward a particular goal, by biasing my behavior toward action.
9. I will use the Core Protocols (or better) when applicable.
   - I will offer and accept timely and proper use of the Core Protocols without prejudice.
10. I will neither harm—nor tolerate the harming of—anyone for his or her fidelity to these commitments.
11. I will never do anything dumb on purpose.

Create Time Yourself

Start by being present. Listen. Share your real self, even at work. Notice the moments when you are tempted to do something dumb on purpose, like complain to the boss or about the boss. Exercise your right to choose rational results-oriented behavior. Choose to use one or more of the tools in this book. Test, try, and experiment. Notice the change in the quality of the time you create.

But be warned. It's no small thing to commit to this list of rules. Being present and engaged in every interaction takes energy and integrity. Entire books have been written just on commitment number two: "I will seek to perceive more than I seek to be perceived." And doing dumb things on purpose seems to be a corporate policy in some organizations. This is a list of rules to be taken seriously.

When it comes to the Core Commitments, accountability in one person isn't enough. Every team member must be accountable to the others, and every team member must be willing to hold the others accountable for their commitments.

Without mutual accountability, "fixing" the team and its transgressions becomes the job of the project manager, HR department, boss, or other external authority. The time-eating monster loves it when bosses and hired guns take over the jobs the team can and should do.

The Core Commitments might be simple, but they are usually not easy. At least at first.

It takes integrity to stand up and say, "We have not shown accountability for the results we promised. We said they would be great and on time, and they're neither. I'm not going to sit back and be mediocre. Will you help me make this great?"

It takes courage to say, "Will you help me with this problem?" when your identity is built on being the expert, being smart, and solving problems.

It takes a belief in oneself to get up and get something done while everyone else stays locked in the meeting, discussion, or argument.

It takes self-awareness not to do something dumb on purpose, even if it's the boss's idea, even if we've always done it, even if the alternative seems scary, and even if everyone else thinks it's the only choice and wants to take action now.

It takes wisdom to ask gracefully what someone's intent was when you're angry.

It's not easy at first, but with practice, it becomes second nature. And the time you claim back from the monster is worth it.

Part 2:

Keep A Toolbox:

The Simple Tools—The Core Protocols

Chapter 1:

Use All the Resources You've Got:

Ask for Help

"If you don't ask, you don't get."

Stevie Wonder

Feeding the Monster

Greg is presenting his proposal to the boss, and you think he's really making a mess of it. The boss is tapping the end of his pen on the table. Three of your colleagues are furiously studying the blank lined paper in their notepads. Greg's voice is getting shaky, and he keeps forgetting what he wants to say next.

Greg told you about his idea last week. You think it's not bad. It needs some work, but it's time he stepped up and took the lead on running this past the decision-makers himself. Now that you're watching him in action, you are sure nothing good is going to come out of this presentation. He's lost in the details, and you wish he'd just get on with selling the idea.

Finally, you can't stand it anymore, and you jump in, giving your take on why the idea is a great one and how you see it moving forward. You are fast, accurate, and precise. You make a pretty good case, you're sure. You hope Greg takes notes for his next presentation. But when you glance at him, he looks furious. And your colleagues are a bit uncomfortable as well. When you're done the boss asks you to follow up with him on next steps, and moves on to the next item on the agenda.

After the meeting, as you're packing up, you congratulate Greg on selling the proposal to the boss.

"What do you mean?" He says, angrily. "It wasn't me, it was you."

"Well, I just helped you tighten the presentation up a bit, that's all," you say.

"No you didn't. You stole it from me. You had to look like the star. Everybody knows that's what you do all the time. That's why no one wants to work on anything with you, because you're always 'helping' them and walking away with all the recognition. I was expecting you to do that. That's why I was so nervous."

And he storms out of the room.

Can you hear the monster breathing? Cleaning up after this episode will feed it for weeks.

We want to help others. In fact, we've been taught that our worth as members of the human community will be measured by how helpful we are. So we offer advice, we secretly do the work of others and surprise them with the finished product, we help people fetch and carry, we clean up after them, we correct their mistakes, we tell them about their faults so they don't have to hear it from others, and we do their work for them so they don't have to.

Why is it that instead of getting thanked for being helpful, sometimes we hear, "I didn't ask for your help!" "Oh, I didn't notice you took out the garbage. Should I have?" and "I wish you'd stop interfering. If I want your help I'll ask for it!"

Where does the disconnect happen? Somewhere between our self-image and theirs. We might want to be seen as helpful. They want to be seen as competent, able, smart, and self-sufficient.

Until you ask for help, you won't hear or accept the help I have to give. I can advise, cajole, admonish, warn, lecture, and hint. You'll find every reason to ignore my advice. The monster loves the time we throw away giving others unsolicited help.

The monster also knows we resist asking for help, so just to make sure we don't get any smart ideas, it encourages us to be "self-sufficient." The result is we just don't ask for help enough. Ever. If you're like most people, you believe the person you ask will think you're whiny or dumb or needy. You are scared you'll be labeled pushy, incompetent, or worse. Here's the news: That's the time-eating monster whispering in your ear.

The monster also appears when you believe only experts can help you with problems on a team. The truth is, most of the problems a team faces are solved simply by talking them through, thinking out loud, sharing, and connecting with others. These are strategies that teams have used for as long as there have been teams.

When we don't ask for help we work in isolation, frustrated and lonely, self-doubt deepening by the hour. We question our own value and wonder at the value of others. After all, why be on a team when you have to do everything yourself? But when we've had our self-sufficient heroic breakthrough, we share our victory with someone, only to have them say, "Why didn't you ask for help? I could have fixed that for you right away and we could have moved forward on more important things."

Next up in the diabolical bag of tricks: when someone asks for help, despite our deep misgivings we listen to the monstrous whisper and say, "Yes, sure, I'll help, no problem."

We lie. When we want to say, "No," we say, "Yes" to feel good about ourselves, to impress others, to repay a debt, or to suck up.

When you say, "Yes," but want to say, "No," it may seem trivial, but over time it eats you alive. You spend time worrying, planning your escape strategy, and dealing with your own ambivalence to the work. The team has to deal with your drama, frustration, and resistance, and then ultimately has to replace you when either you give up or they ask you to leave.

WHAT GREAT TEAMS DO

Great teams have a thriving culture of asking for help. It's a way of getting the next breakthrough, connecting with other team members, seeing a new perspective, or solving a problem.

One sign of a great team is a casual and easy-going exchange of requests and help. A team is getting into trouble when requests for help dry up. A team in deep trouble stands out with its formal meetings and facilitated intervention. The monster thrives on large group discussion and process-based intervention.

Great teams ask for help at all levels. As individuals, they ask each other. As subteams within the larger team, they seek out passionate people who care about their work to join them and add value. As teams, they ask for help from other teams working on both similar and completely different work.

Great teams also ask for help boundlessly, focusing more on the potential value of the help than on organizational boundaries, hierarchy, or even industry. I might ask for help from someone in a different department because she's simply a good thinker. I might connect with an acquaintance in another industry over social media, knowing she will have an insight or question that opens up a new perspective.

Each person respects that every team mate is smart enough to know when he needs help and smart enough to ask. Giving help on a team like this isn't about showing how helpful or smart you are. It's about moving the action forward. It might be another set of hands, or the opportunity to think out loud without competition, expectation, and judgment. It might be a genuinely different perspective that may open up the problem to new analysis. And that moves the team forward to its goals.

Really great teams ask for help at all times, good and bad, knowing that the improvement they get from each other's help when they are struggling will result in a shift to goodness. Therefore, if they start with help when things are good, they'll get to magnificent.

Team members are also open to an alternative to what they asked for. "Will you help me write this article?" could be answered, "No, but I'll copyedit it when you have a draft finished. Would you like me to do that?"

And finally, great teams take "No" for an answer. For people to make a habit of asking for help as often as it's useful, the person asked must have the freedom to say, "No." That freedom comes from mutually committing to accepting "No" as an answer without arguing, questioning, wheedling, or accusing. "No" is ok when you can ask anyone for help any time.

Great teams know no one knows where good ideas will come from, so they don't limit whom to ask.

THE CORE PROTOCOL

Ask For Help

The Ask For Help protocol allows you to efficiently make use of the skills and knowledge of others. Ask For Help is the act that catalyzes connection and shared vision. Use it continuously, before and during the pursuit of any result.

STEPS

1. Asker inquires of another, "[Helper's name], will you X?"
2. Asker expresses any specifics or restrictions of the request.
3. Helper responds by saying, "Yes" or "No" or by offering an alternative form of help.

COMMITMENTS

- Always invoke the Ask For Help protocol with the phrase "Will you..."

- Have a clear understanding of what you want from the helper. Or if you do not have a clear understanding of what help you want, signal this by saying, "I'm not sure what I need help with, but will you help me?"
- Assume that all Helpers are always available, and trust that any Helper accepts the responsibility to say, "No."
- Say, "No" any time you do not want to help.
- Accept the answer "No" without any inquiry or emotional drama.
- Be receptive of the help offered.
- Offer your best help even if it is not what the Asker is expecting.
- Postpone the help request if you are unable to fully engage.
- Request more information if you are unclear about the specifics of the help request.
- Do not apologize for asking for help.

NOTES

- Asking for help is a low-cost undertaking. The worst possible outcome is a "No," which leaves you no farther ahead or behind than when you asked. In the best possible outcome, you reduce the amount of time required to achieve a task and/or learn.

- Helpers should say, "No" if they are not sure if they want to help. They should say nothing else after turning down a request for help.
- You cannot "over ask" a given person for help unless he or she has asked you to respect a particular limit.
- If you don't understand the value of what is offered, or feel that it wouldn't be useful, or believe yourself to have considered and rejected the idea offered previously, assume a curious stance instead of executing a knee-jerk "But..." rejection. (See the Investigate protocol.)
- Asking in time of trouble means you waited too long to Ask For Help. Ask For Help when you are doing well.
- Simply connecting with someone, even if he or she knows nothing of the subject you need help on, can help you find answers within yourself, especially if you ask that person to Investigate you.

CREATE TIME YOURSELF

Think of something you've been working on lately. It could be a work project, a relationship that you want to mend, or a strategy on how to increase community participation in local schools.

Go to three people you don't normally ask for help—like the sales guy in the next cubicle, your mother, and your peer in another department. Share the protocol with them, and make sure they know they can say, "No." Then ask them for help. Remember, don't argue! Just thank them and move on.

If you're on a team, the next step is to ask each person on the team to try that exercise and share what they learned.

Ask each other, whether on your team, in your family, or in your community. Ask when you think you don't have to, when you've got it all under control. And then ask some more.

Start saying, "No" when you're asked for help. Say, "No" just to practice saying, "No." When you model that behavior, it makes it safe for others to say, "No" as well.

I've heard objections about asking for help from people who have never tried it, like, "Won't people just ask for other people's help to avoid doing their own work?" or "Won't the helpful people end up doing everything?"

My answer to them is, "Follow the protocol and give it a try. Assume others are smart and have good intentions. Say, 'No' when you want to say, 'No.' Offer alternatives without insisting on them."

And a final suggestion, but one that may lead to world peace: Ask your partner, spouse, kids, parents, or significant other to help you with household chores. Don't whine, demand, shame, expect, or excuse. Just ask for help.

Be specific: "Will you take all the dirty laundry from all the bedrooms and bathrooms, sort it into light and dark, put the light clothes in the laundry machine, and leave the rest in sorted piles on the floor?"

Assume they're smart and have good intentions, so if they do something you wouldn't do, maybe they have a different level of experience, skill, or knowledge. Or maybe, just maybe, they have a better idea about how to do the laundry! Fix the problem, not them. And thank them when they're done.

Chapter 2:

Be A No-Feedback Zone: Investigate

"Advice is like castor oil, easy enough to give but dreadful uneasy to take."

Josh Billings

Feeding the Monster

Anita and Carla meet for coffee.

Anita, clearly troubled, says, "I really don't know what to think about the boss's comments yesterday."

Carla says, "Here's some feedback: You are too sensitive. You need to get a thicker skin. Don't let him bother you like that. You'll never make director letting things like that get to you."

Anita is speechless. Based on one brief statement, Carla has made an series of assumptions: What it is Anita's worried about, whether there is fault, what she should do about it, Anita's contribution to the problem, and how Anita received it. None of these assumptions are correct. But the very worst assumption was that Anita wanted feedback.

Anita is angry that she hasn't been heard, afraid that she missed something even bigger than what she's already worried about, and sad that she can't find anyone to just listen instead of trying to fix problems they don't understand. She's also angry that she had to take feedback she didn't ask for, especially when Carla didn't even understand what Anita was concerned about.

Now the time-eating monster will get a free lunch on Anita's new worries, her old worries that haven't been resolved, and the new tension between Anita and Carla, which will spill over into the work they do together.

Carla, like most of us in this situation, gave feedback because she genuinely wanted to help. She had a solution waiting for a problem, and when Anita opened her mouth, Carla played the game many of us play unconsciously every day: Have the answer and give feedback. It feels good to tell others what they need to do better.

But what if we're wrong? What if the person we've given feedback to wasn't ready for it? Or she didn't need help at all, but wanted to work things through herself? Or she would have asked for a completely different kind of help in the course of the conversation, but won't now that you've done your preemptive feedback strike?

Feedback requires a whole load of assumptions. For me to give you feedback, I have to assume I have feedback that is valuable, that I can communicate in a way that you will understand and be able to use, that you want feedback, that you're in the right mindset to receive it, and that it will amplify your actions and not damp them.

Feedback also becomes a crutch in power relationships. Let's put aside the theoretical workplace for a moment. In most workplaces, communities, and families, if you're my boss, director, or parent, I have learned that I must accept your feedback to keep your favor or remain employed.

In fact, boss feedback is built right into most human resources plans, and it is titled performance appraisal. In families, feedback tends to show up in less formal ways. It's part of the exchange in any power relationship. I pay you, praise you, or feed and clothe you, usually on behalf of the larger organization, and you do what I ask. If you're not doing what I ask, and I give you feedback on what I want to see instead, it would be wise for you to take note of what I suggest as an alternative. We call this a "performance appraisal" in most organizations.

On the other hand, if you're my employee, volunteer, or child, I don't have to accept your feedback. I would, of course, be wise to do so, but there is no reciprocal performance appraisal for the boss in most organizations. At best, a good boss will take employee feedback under consideration. At worst, it's a firing offense. In between is a messy, time-wasting mix of resentment, payback, sabotage, and gossip.

Peer feedback is an interesting case. And this is where great teams excel. The peer-feedback scenario often plays itself out in public, in those familiar business meetings. Everyone speaks. Over, under, in agreement, with cynicism, distain, sarcasm, veiled contempt—barely touching the nominal topic. When the meeting is over, the room is barely large enough to contain the monster as it feeds.

How Great Teams Create Time

Putting aside, for now, the formal feedback processes used in some organizations today, feedback, in the loose way most organizations use the term, really means "telling her something about herself that will make her stop doing something I don't like." Feedback in the form of unsolicited advice is almost guaranteed to spawn monsters.

On great teams that already have a thriving culture of asking for help, feedback for this reason or any other is really unnecessary. If I am always asking for ideas, thoughts, help, and value from you and others, you will rarely if ever feel the need to offer unsolicited advice. I will have already figured out what will work well for everyone, made a choice, and moved on.

Here's where a great team takes things to the next level: If you and I are on a great team, and I ask for your help with a problem, your first response is not to give me the answer. Your first response is to ask me a question. You are genuinely curious. This is a fascinating moment for you. It's a moment in time in a complex system in which an infinite number of possible solutions exist, and the best of those are locked up in my brain. You are fascinated by what solution is the best one, and you know the only way to find out is to ask me questions that unlock the answer. You have a lifetime of solutions at your fingertips, but what you really want is the solutions you haven't seen yet.

Asking each other open questions might possibly be the greatest time-creation tool we have.

THE CORE PROTOCOL

Investigate

The Investigate Protocol allows you to learn about a phenomenon that occurs in someone else. Use it when an idea or behavior someone is presenting seems poor, confusing, or simply interesting.

STEPS

1. Act as if you were a detached but fascinated inquirer, asking questions until your curiosity is satisfied or you no longer want to ask questions.

COMMITMENTS

- Ask well-formed questions.
- Ask only questions that will increase your understanding.
- Ask questions only if the subject is engaged and appears ready to answer more.
- Refrain from offering opinions.
- Do not ask leading questions where you think you know how he or she will answer.

- If you cannot remain a detached, curious investigator with no agenda, stop using the protocol until you can come back to it and keep these commitments.

NOTES

- Do not theorize about the subject or provide any sort of diagnosis.
- Consider using the following forms for your questions:
  - ✓ What about X makes you Z?
  - ✓ Would you explain a specific example?
  - ✓ How does X go when it happens?
  - ✓ What is the one thing you want most from solving X?
  - ✓ What is the biggest problem you see regarding X now?
  - ✓ What is the most important thing you could do right now to help you with X?
- Ineffective queries include the following:
  - ✓ Questions that lead or reflect an agenda.
  - ✓ Questions that attempt to hide an answer you believe is true.
  - ✓ Questions that invite stories.
  - ✓ Questions that begin with "Why."
- Stick to your intention of gathering more information.
- If you feel that you will explode if you can't say what's on your mind, you shouldn't speak at

all. Consider checking your intention or Check Out.

Create Time Yourself

First, Practice Asking Questions

In a casual setting, such as the next time you're having coffee with a friend or partner, try limiting yourself to only questions. From a genuine place of curiosity, as if they were a fascinating stranger or even a celebrity you've just met, ask them about their experiences, what's important to them, and what they like.

The best questions you can ask are open questions that have no agenda and to which you don't know the answer. Questions that start with "What" are perfect. For instance, instead of "Don't you think you should..." or, "Isn't it true that..." ask, "What could you do if..." or "What have you thought about so far?"

Avoid "Why," which sounds like a parent. Unless you were a model teenager, "Why didn't you call me when you were going to be late?" should raise some uncomfortable associations. Assume the same is true for your equally complex peer. Questions that will result in "Yes" or "No" are junk food for the brain, questions a computer could have asked. Instead, ask questions worthy of someone who is smart, present, interested, and engaged. Ask questions worthy of your time and hers.

If you are desperate to give the person advice, it's even more imperative that you stick to questions, because it is likely you've stopped listening. When you can't help yourself, it's time to go.

Next, Ask Others to Investigate You

Ask someone else for help with a problem, decision, challenge, or quandary. For instance, say, "Will you ask me questions you have about this decision I want to make?" or "Will you Investigate me on this problem I'm having with my boss?" Be sure you don't use the experience as a way to complain, whine, or get sympathy. As soon as you do that, the time-eating monster slips into the space and settles in. The goal is for you to find the answer in yourself, so you need to remain as present and curious as your partner.

Because we are all taught to be experts in each other's life, and they probably care about you and your welfare, it's likely your questioner will unintentionally ask leading questions. Those are the ones that start with "Don't you think..." and "Are you sure that..." and "Couldn't you..." If they accidentally ask leading questions like these, gently remind them the questions need to be open and non-directive for you to get the most out of the conversation. And thank them for helping you slay the time-eating monster.

Chapter 3:

Share Mad, Sad, Glad, and Afraid: Check In

"Emotions have taught mankind to reason."

Marquis De Vauvenarques

Feeding the Monster

You fight with traffic to get to work, the windshield wipers break in the snowstorm, and the last parking space is in a lake of icy mush. The first thing you have to do once you squelch your way into the office is attend a meeting about the project schedule. The time-eating monster is already pleased and whispering in your ear that you soldier on "for the good of the team" and get through the meeting.

You try to hide your foul mood, but it keeps coming out as snarky comments and heavy sighs. You're getting as mad at yourself as you are about everything else. Your colleagues fidget, placate you, and do their best to pretend nothing's wrong. The monster silently salivates.

You find out three days later that your colleague was scared you were mad at her, and she's been tiptoeing around you for days. And one of your direct reports had an idea in the meeting that would save the company thousands by consolidating suppliers, but he thought you were mad at him for something he had done last week (he's not sure what) so he kept it to himself.

The monster waits to see what other entirely avoidable misunderstandings will show up on the time-eating buffet.

When we turned to machines to do work for us, we got an idea that since machines were unemotional and efficient it would make humans efficient to be unemotional. So for decades we've been training each other to "leave our emotions at the door." In fact, we've become so convinced that emotions are below us and unnecessary, most of us don't even know what we or anyone else is feeling.

In the greatest case of willful blindness in our corporate world, we think that if we don't acknowledge emotions at work, they will go away. The truth is the pressure has built up so much that we're leaking emotion all the time like a garden hose, and it's getting our work all wet.

Hidden fear drives many decisions we make at work. We fear losing power, of making mistakes, being ridiculed, or being exposed as a fraud. Suppressed anger costs millions in turnover and lost opportunity. Sadness over loss in our personal and professional lives leads to sick days and depression. And the rare time we feel joy at work must be smothered as well, in case our colleagues think we are unprofessional.

Humans are wired to have emotions, to use communication to share those emotions, and to use emotion to get results. Emotions inform and guide everything we do as individuals and as team members, and we can't hide them no matter how tightly we squeeze. Those leaky emotions cost us time, and more and more time disappears to the monster's insatiable appetite the longer and harder we try to bottle them up.

How Great Teams Create Time

Great teams acknowledge that humans get great things done, and at the same time acknowledge that humans are complex, adaptive systems. Emotions are part of who we are. We can't make emotions go away as if they were error messages on our computer screens. In fact, great teams know that emotions can give us valuable clues about how to behave, what action we should take, and what is important in the mental and physical space we share with others.

For instance, if I'm angry about something, that's usually a clue that there's a problem somewhere. Perhaps a commitment has been broken, a possibility is being missed, or there's a roadblock somewhere. If I can effectively notice, acknowledge, and figure out the cause of my anger, I can ask for help to fix the problem.

I can also share the causes of my emotions with others in a neutral way so they don't have to wonder about my behavior. If I share that I'm mad because my feet are wet and cold, then my teammates know I'm not mad because I think they screwed up. Or, if I screw up and say I'm mad because of that, it opens a door of honesty through which I can ask for help. Hiding that feeling keeps the door tightly shut.

On great teams, individuals reveal their feelings in a simple, neutral exchange. Without drama, I can let you know why I seem distracted, easily irritated, or distant. I can even use that revelation to open up a request to you to Investigate me, to help resolve an issue, or to help me get something done. But that extension is at my discretion.

Most importantly, I don't tell you how I feel so that you will rescue me, feel guilty about it, or offer advice. You don't need to respond or feel empathy or sympathy. The miracle is simply your trusted presence.

And then I recommit to the Core Commitments.

THE CORE PROTOCOL

Check In

Use the Check In protocol to begin meetings or anytime an individual or group Check In would add more value to the current team interactions.

STEPS

1. Speaker says, "I feel [mad, sad, glad, afraid, or a combination]." Speaker may provide a brief explanation. Or if others have already checked in, Speaker may say, "I pass." (See the Pass protocol.)
2. Speaker says, "I'm in." This signifies Speaker intends to behave according to the Core Commitments.

3. Listeners respond, "Welcome."

COMMITMENTS

- State feelings without qualification.
- State feelings only as they pertain to yourself.
- Be silent during another's Check In.
- Do not refer to another's Check In disclosures without explicitly gaining permission from him or her.

NOTES

- In the context of the Core Protocols, all emotions are expressed through combinations of mad, sad, glad, and afraid. For example, excited may be a combination of glad and afraid.
- Check In as deeply as possible. Checking in with two or more emotions is the norm. The depth of a group's Check In translates directly to the quality of the group's results.
- Do not do anything to diminish your emotional state. Do not describe yourself as a "little" mad, sad, glad, or afraid, or say, "I'm mad, but I'm still glad."
- Except in large groups, if more than one person checks in, it is recommended that all do so.
- Happy may be substituted for glad, and scared may be substituted for afraid.

CREATE TIME YOURSELF

If you're in power, or working with someone in power, the Check In protocol can be a useful tool to avoid fighting and turf wars. Checking In requires vulnerability, something most people in power have been taught never to show. That's a shame, because vulnerability shows a high level of power. The tribal part of our brain does a quick calculation: A person willing to show vulnerability obviously doesn't worry about her power. If the powerful person isn't worried about her power, I don't have to be either.

Revealing emotions is also useful with a rational boss. If I can be vulnerable, it implies I'm willing not to challenge him, at least for the moment. With a strong boss, that can create an opening for a conversation that moves beyond who has the power, and instead allow the discussion to be more cooperative.

The Check In protocol requires a high level of presence to know exactly which of the four emotions we are feeling. Sometimes fear or sadness feel like anger, for instance. Over time and with practice, thinking and speaking about feelings becomes easier and more useful.

The best place to start Checking In is with people you work with regularly: Your boss, team, or peers. They have seen your habits and are already very familiar with your emotional reactions. In fact, you may be surprised how aware they already are that you're feeling something. We all assume others are more transparent and simple than we are, and we tend to attribute characteristics to others based on their observable behavior. And of course others assume the same of us, although we know intimately the complex interior world that leads to the behavior others see in us.

Since they see only your behavior and not your interior experience, your team members will welcome a shortcut to understanding what is emotionally behind how you're behaving, and they will especially welcome a short explanation of why you're feeling that way. They will be relieved to give up being coached by the time-eating monster, who usually recommends second-guessing, sarcasm, tiptoeing, being "nice" while you're in a bad mood, or avoiding you—all of which become irritating after a very short time.

Next, build the foundation of a great team before you start working together, and Check In with people you will be working with in future. We do this in preliminary meetings with our clients, even if they have never heard of the Core Protocols. We simply start meetings by saying something like, "I'm glad I can contribute to the progress of this team, I'm sad I'm away from my family and home, I'm afraid I won't say my best ideas, and I'm mad that I can't get Internet connectivity to download the latest file."

We Check In while working, at transitions between work and other activities, and with family.

Check In when you're about to have a meeting, particularly one that may be emotionally charged. Then Check In if something changes in that meeting. For instance, if you realize a project will be delivered late, you could Check In that you're mad you weren't on schedule and you intend to be more aware in the next iteration. Or you can use the Ask For Help protocol, and ask the team what will be different next time. Remember to be accountable for your own feelings. Never blame someone else for how you're feeling.

The Check In protocol is very simple and fast, and it precludes the water cooler conversations that inevitably happen after a meeting with the new person: "Didn't you think she looked angry all through the meeting? Wonder who pissed in her cornflakes?"

Chapter 4:

Claim Your Freedom to Leave: Check Out

"No problem is so formidable that you can't walk away from it."

Charles M. Schulz

Feeding the Monster

"You really messed this one up!" he says to you, in front of the rest of the managers. "Did you think no one would notice?"

You are furious. It's one thing to criticise yourself. It's entirely different when someone else criticizes you in front of the team. You fight back, finding all the reasons he was as responsible for the outcome as you, taking up the meeting time with what you believe is a righteous self-defense. You won't let him win this.

Your accuser is delighting in your emotional outburst; it supports his campaign to replace you. The junior members of the team are sitting with their arms crossed, hoping no one will notice them. Senior members play with their pencils or do email, waiting until it all blows over.

After ten minutes of emotional brinksmanship, your adversary is satisfied.

"Well," he says. "Would you like to grow up now, or shall we reschedule the meeting?"

You come close to starting up the fight all over again, but you contain yourself just in time. Your temper is up, and you've lost all functioning in your rational brain. But you don't want to seem to give up or make a scene by leaving. So you stew through the meeting, snarky and critical, snapping at every comment regardless of its value. You are distracting everyone, including yourself, and the distraction will last for days. Time seems to be rushing by your ears into the jaws of the monster.

How Great Teams Create Time

On great teams, butts in seats aren't interesting, effort isn't interesting, and suffering is certainly not interesting. When someone is suffering and showing it by being short tempered, sarcastic, distracted, or anxious, great teams are thankful that the person leaves and goes to get what they need to come back ready to work.

As we've seen from the Check In protocol as well, suppressing the emotion is not the answer. Emotion is real, and every individual's emotional state is a part of the system. However, when emotions become overwhelming, they can become attractors for the attention of the team, distracting the team from the work they need to do.

A great team supports its members' freedom to leave. Without making the simple rule of commitment to rational behavior, we are tempted to stay when we should really leave, and to provide unsolicited help to someone if only to ease our own suffering in the presence of theirs.

So great teams support each other in Checking Out. Each person knows they'll want to Check Out someday. Supporting someone else, or practicing it and modeling it, creates an environment in which everyone can get a chance.

THE CORE PROTOCOL

Check Out

The Check Out protocol requires that your physical presence always signifies your engagement. You must Check Out when you are aware that you cannot maintain the Core Commitments, or whenever it would be better for you to be elsewhere.

STEPS

1. Say, "I'm checking out."
2. Physically leave the group until you're ready to Check In once again.
3. Optionally, if it is known and relevant, you can say when you believe you'll return.
4. Those who are present for the Check Out may not follow the person, talk to or about the person checking out, or otherwise chase him or her.

COMMITMENTS

- Return as soon as you can and are able to keep the Core Commitments.
- Return and Check In without unduly calling attention to your return.
- Do not judge, shame, hassle, interrogate, or punish anyone who checks out.

NOTES

- When you Check Out, do it as calmly and gracefully as possible so as to cause minimal disruption to others.
- Check Out if your emotional state is hindering your success, if your receptivity to new information is too low, or if you do not know what you want.
- Check Out is an admission that you are unable to contribute at the present time.

CREATE TIME YOURSELF

The next time you notice you are exhausted, tense, overwhelmed, or getting close to being overwhelmed, try saying, "I'm feeling like I'm not able to contribute here. I'm going to Check Out for a bit, and I'll come back when I've thought more about the issue."

If you're still rational, the best thing to do is get out of the team's space and ask someone for help, one-to-one. Like every use of the Ask For Help protocol, it creates connection, brings a new perspective, and builds trust. And while you're getting those things, the team can continue working without being distracted.

However, when you're beyond being rational—too angry, tired, fearful, or sad to think straight—the best thing you can do is get out of the team's space and get some time alone.

A great signal to yourself that you need to Check Out is when you say or do in public what you otherwise would keep to yourself. Saying it isn't wrong, but saying it skillfully while in a rational state of mind will get much better results.

We all get tired, caregivers more so than others. If you're a parent or are caring for someone, have an emergency backup preplanned for the times when you have to Check Out. Maybe a neighbor, friend, or relative could come and temporarily take your place while you get what you need.

It's also important to have a list of ways you can get what you need in order to return to the team gracefully. For me, taking a walk, doing exercise, or sleeping are often all I need to reset my system. If I start feeling overwhelmingly angry, sad, or afraid, I will often go for a fast walk right away. When I feel I'm ready, I return to the team space and check with the team to see if anything has changed while I've been gone.

I find that often my own tension was a barrier to progress for the team. By removing myself from the space, they have had breathing room to shift their focus off me and back onto the work, and while I was gone they've moved forward.

Chapter 5:

Know and Get What You Want: Personal Alignment

"I always wanted to be somebody, but now I realize I should have been more specific. "

Lily Tomlin

Feeding the Monster

I want things. Some of those things are tangible, like more money, or a promotion, a long-term relationship, or better health. Some of those things, though, are less tangible, like wanting to be more comfortable in social situations, wanting to be more present or self-aware, or wanting to live more joyfully.

I may also want very practical things. I want to speak up when I see a problem, or share ideas with the team, or ask for help from someone who intimidates me, or get support for something I'm working on that I'm proud of.

The monster is particularly dastardly when it comes to what we want. It whispers in familiar tones that those things are "personal," and they aren't appropriate to share with the people I work with. It says that my teammates won't want to spend time on "my stuff." When I hear myself saying, "I don't want to be pushy and selfish," "They're all really busy, and I don't want to interrupt them," or "This is my own thing, and I have to work it out myself," I can smell the dry, musty presence of the beast.

It wants me to waste time in isolation as much as I want the things I want. If I'm not careful, it will win.

The monster has us all convinced that it's also not appropriate to spend time at work having personal concerns and goals, so we try to keep work and "not work" separate. If you're like me, it makes you mad that you believe you have to create this separation. After all, you're the same person wherever you are. But in the monster's world only a small piece of you walks in the door every morning.

An industry has grown to produce idealistic motivational posters and other products to reinforce this disconnected vision of people at work. These products promote messages like "There's no 'I' in team." Just as quickly another industry has grown, even more popular than the original, that parodies silly propaganda like that.

The parodies are more popular because people recognize how unrealistic and limiting the half-human view of teamwork is. Trying to ignore personal concerns at work is like pretending you have no past or future. And the boundaries we artificially create to achieve half-human status limit the intimacy a team needs to build time-creating trust.

Every person brings his or her whole self to every context, whether it's welcome there or not. I can't stop myself from thinking about my vacation, my kids, or my sick relative when I'm at work. And I can't stop myself from thinking about work when I'm somewhere else.

If part of what I have and what I am is unwelcome, and only part of me can be applied to a task, it's no surprise the products and services we create and consume are so mediocre. The energy of the team was spent not on creating something fantastic for the organization's customers, but on trying so hard to be hidden and only half present. The banquet begins for the fiend when we spend time deliberately on *not* getting results.

HOW GREAT TEAMS CREATE TIME

Great teams know each team member must be able to bring all of himself or herself to every part of his or her lives if the products they create will be great.

Great teams are made up of whole humans who are passionate about their own dreams and ambitions and those of the team as a whole. They use that passion, connection, and trust as rocket fuel for delivering great results. In most cases, the members of a great team are on the team precisely because it supports their integrity and authenticity.

We will all get what we want eventually or ruin ourselves in an effort not to. If I want to create something I'm passionate about and I have to keep it to myself, it's likely I'll steal time from work to make it happen. I'll come in late, leave early, work on it during office hours, and take sick days to get it done.

But if I don't have to hide my passion and excitement about my achievement, it becomes fuel for the team. It feeds them. And that energy rebounds within the web of the team, lighting up passion and energy in everyone else. That passion and energy is poison to the monster.

Supporting each other to achieve personal goals builds passion and energy to collectively reach the team's goals. Helping each other in all contexts reinforces helping each other in specific contexts. We say the team equals the product. Whatever is true of the team is true of what they create, whether what they create is a product, service, organization, or another team.

The Core Protocol

Personal Alignment

The Personal Alignment protocol helps you penetrate deeply into your desires and find what's blocking you from getting what you want. Use it to discover, articulate, and achieve what you want. The quality of your alignment will be equal to the quality of your results.

Steps

1. Want. Answer the question, "What specifically do I want?"
2. Block. Ask yourself, "What is blocking me from having what I want?"
3. Virtue. Figure out what would remove this block by asking yourself, "What virtue—if I had it—would shatter this block of mine?"
4. Shift. Pretend the virtue you identified is actually what you want.

5. Again. Repeat steps two to four until this process consistently yields a virtue that is powerful enough to shatter your blocks and get you what you originally thought you wanted.
6. Done. Now write down a personal-alignment statement in the form "I want [virtue]." For example, "I want courage."
7. Signal/Response/Assignment. Create a signal to let others know when you are practicing your alignment, and provide a response they can give you to demonstrate support. For example, "When I say or do X, will you say or do Y?" Optionally, turn it into an assignment by saying you will do X a certain number of times per day, where X equals an activity that requires you to practice living your alignment.
8. Evidence. Write, in specific and measurable terms, the long-term evidence of practicing this alignment.
9. Help. Ask each member of your group for help. They help by giving the response you would like when you give your signal that you are practicing your alignment.

COMMITMENTS

- Identify an alignment that will result in your personal change and require no change from any other person.

- Identify blocks and wants that are specific and personal.
- Identify blocks that, if solved, would radically increase your effectiveness in life, work, and play.
- Choose a virtue that is about you, preferably one word long. For example, choose integrity, passion, self-care, peace, or fun.
- Ask For Help from people who know you and/or know alignments.
- Identify evidence that is measurable by an objective third party.

NOTES

- The most popular personal alignments are "I want (Integrity, Courage, Passion, Peace, Self-Awareness, Self-Care)".
- If you are struggling with figuring out what you want, adopt the alignment "I want self-awareness." There is no case where increased self-awareness would not be beneficial.
- A personal block is something you find within yourself. It does not refer to circumstances or other people. Assume that you could have had what you want by now, and that your block is a myth that somehow deprives you of your full potential.
- Ideally, identify both immediate and long-term evidence of your alignment. Write down results that start now (or very soon), as well as results

you'll see at least five or more years in the future.

- As a default signal, tell your teammates or others who are close to you that you are working on your alignment when you are practicing it. If they don't know the protocol, just tell them what virtue you are working on and ask for their help.
- When members of a team are completing their personal alignments together (asking each other for help), the final step of the process is most powerful if done as a ceremony.

CREATE TIME YOURSELF

Working on your personal alignment has a personal part and a shared part. The personal part you can do on your own. The shared part requires a little help from your friends.

The Personal Alignment protocol benefits from two other protocols to really make it work. The first is the Ask For Help protocol, and the second is the Investigate protocol.

So, make sure you read through the chapters on those two protocols first, and then come back here. This might be your first taste of how all the tools work together.

Here's the personal part. Now that you've read through the Ask For Help protocol and the Investigate protocol, think about what you want. That means what you want out of your entire life. Lots of people start with what they want from work, like a higher salary, more responsibility, a change of workplace, or work on a different team. Then, if they have other things they want, they add those in too. For instance, you might want to travel to every continent, or take cooking lessons, or save for your child's education, or get healthy. Wherever you start and end is fine, as long as it means something to you. Quantity isn't important. What's important is that where you're going is worth the work you're going to put into it.

Once you've got an idea of something you want, you're going to combine three protocols: You'll use the Ask For Help protocol and what you're going to ask for is that someone Investigate you about your Personal Alignment.

Find someone you trust and tell them you're trying this new way to figure out what you want and how to get it. Show them the Investigate protocol, and ask them if they would be willing to be a curious questioner, remaining unattached to the outcome of your conversation. Then share what you want with them. Ask them to Investigate whatever they are curious about, like what it is that's important to you about your goal.

If you're comfortable with the conversation about what you want, then ask them to Investigate what virtue would help you get what you want. Some people call it a quality. It's not necessarily something missing in you. It's often something you already have, and turning up the volume on it to drown out the other distractions will give you the edge to break through what's blocking you from having what you want today.

Only you know what virtue you want to work on. Everyone is starting from a unique place, a combination of thousands of variables that have stacked up over the years. So a goal you think needs an alignment of courage for you might need an alignment of integrity for someone else. For instance, if you look at the news about New Year's resolutions in early January, who doesn't want to get healthier? But the quality each person brings to that want will be different. I might need to master self-care to get healthy. But you, already masterful with self-care but losing interest in it, might need to turn up the volume on fun to get your mojo back.

So when you Ask For Help with the virtue you choose, remind your Investigator that they don't have to figure out the answer for you—that's your job. All they have to do is be curious and ask questions. You know what you need but have lost track of it, and they are there to help you find it again.

Write down what you want, what will help you get it, and what outcomes you'll have because you worked on it. Put calendar dates to each outcome so you and others can keep you accountable to your goals. The more measurable your goal, the more likely it is you'll achieve it. Write down your evidence in terms of having achieved it.

For instance, write, "By June 30, 20XX I will have completed the Boston Marathon at least once." Or write, "By August 15, 20XX, I will have delivered the keynote address at the Annual Conference of the Society of Really Cool People." Or even, "By the end of this month I will have read a bedtime story to my child at least three times per week."

Visualizing your goals as if they have been achieved makes them real in your mind and helps you more clearly figure out what milestones you need to reach along the way. Write those down too! Soon you'll have a plan for achieving what you want.

But you're not finished. In fact, you've just started.

You need more help. You need support, reinforcement, and people to talk to who know what you're trying to achieve. This is where your team comes in again. Ask them to bear witness to your success or your integrity in working toward your goal. Ask them to pump you up when you did something challenging or hit a milestone. They will ask you for help in return. Ask as many people as you can to Investigate you, and Investigate others when they ask you to. Every time you and others talk about your alignments, it becomes clearer, more concrete, and familiar. The connections on the team become stronger.

You'll also have a whole army of people invested in your progress. They may even expect you to report back periodically with your milestones and achievements in hand. Having that support and interest is powerful in helping us stay accountable to our own big picture. The qualities of each person seeking his or her own best self will roll up into the qualities of the team, the qualities of its products, and of the organization it works for.

In the process of helping each other get what you want as individuals, a web of connections in the team will emerge. It will be the most comprehensive tool in the toolbox for slaying the time-eating monster. So much time is saved on a team that has a robust web of support and trust, it seems sometimes like you have a time machine. Compared to other teams, you create time at will.

Chapter 6:

Check Intent Early and Often: Intention Check

"It is wiser to find out than to suppose."

Mark Twain

Feeding the Monster

You're lying awake thinking about the conversation at work. You're still fuming. And of course, the time-eating monster is calculating all the time it'll get to eat for the next few days.

You and Jack were working on the proposal for the new account. You had packed up for the day, and just as he left the room, Jack said, "Well, it's a good thing you won't be on this account much longer." And he was gone.

You were stunned. What did he mean by that?

You started the play-by-play analysis, going over every conversation you'd had in the past three months. Had you done something career limiting? Angered the boss? Said something wrong to the customer? You wonder about every interaction and every email. Your confidence was shaken, which then got you mad. You fumed all night about Jack's attitude, coldly going through the list of his faults one after the other. Finally, you chewed on the possibility that a pink slip would be waiting when you got to work the next day.

Now, you get to work, sweating and nervous, exhausted from the sleepless night. No pink slip is waiting. You say, "Good morning," to your peers and watch their expressions for any clues. Does anyone else know something?

This goes on for days. You're distracted, short-tempered, and defensive. Work is piling up. You haven't heard any more about the new account, and you're afraid to ask. You are avoiding Jack, though he seems indifferent. You start checking the job boards just in case. The monster is delighted things are going exactly the way it planned.

After a week, Jack finally says, "Hey, you seem a bit tired. What's up?"

You freeze, then take a deep breath and remind him of what happened. He stares at you, stunned.

"Have you been worrying about that?" He says with a smile. "Haven't you heard about the big new project coming down the pipe? They want you to work on that instead of this piddly, little, go-nowhere account. I heard the boss talking about it. I figured you knew."

Count up the hours you spend thinking about the things others say and the things you never ask them about in the moment. At dinner, watching the movie, reading your email, playing with your kids, at 3:00 a.m. with the sheets bunched in your fists. What's your time worth? You do the math. The monster certainly knows.

How Great Teams Create Time

Great teams regularly use a simple tool to Check Intent. They never assume. You may have been hurt by what he said, but did he intend to hurt you? How you deal with his comment can depend (a lot) on the answer. So great teams simply ask, "What was your intent?" and wait calmly for the answer.

On great teams, because each person is committed (remember the Core Commitments?) to being present, as well as offering and accepting rational, results-oriented behavior, if a team member feels emotionally overwhelmed and wants to Check Intent, they will Check Out first. That way, they can come back in a rational state of mind before asking the question.

But they do ask, and that's the key. Ask early, and ask often.

The Core Protocol

Intention Check

Use the Intention Check protocol to clarify the purpose of your own or another's behavior. Use it when you aren't expecting a positive outcome resulting from the current behavior. The Intention Check protocol assesses the integrity of your own and another's intention in a given case.

Steps

1. Ask, "What is your/my intention with X?" where X equals some type of actual or pending behavior to the person whose intention you want to know.
2. If it would be helpful, ask, "What response or behavior did you want from whom as X?"

Commitments

- Be aware of your own intention before checking the intention of another.
- Investigate sufficiently to uncover the intention of the person or his actions.
- Make sure you have the intention to resolve any possible conflict peacefully before checking someone else's intention. If you do not have a peaceful intention, Check Out.
- Do not be defensive when someone asks you what your intention is. If you can't do this, Check Out.

Notes

- If conflict arises that seems irresolvable, use the Check Out and Ask For Help protocols.

Create Time Yourself

When someone says something that seems uncharacteristic or counterproductive, especially if it affects your trust in them, start with the assumption of good intent and intelligence. Ask yourself, "If this person has good intent and is smart, what would cause them to behave this way?"

When you're able to be truly curious, and you are ready to really hear what the true intent was without suspicion, follow the protocol. Try it in neutral situations first, just to get the hang of it.

Don't add anything to the question. Stay away from blame, accusation, or questions of how they hurt you. They may have been unskillful in the way they said it, or the context may have been wrong, or there was a language translation problem. Or they may have intended to be hurtful. But you'll never know if you leapfrog the protocol and get in a fight in the first few seconds.

This tool can be especially helpful with teenagers, parents, and siblings. Checking intent explicitly can save years of heartbreak from misunderstanding.

It's easy to react to something someone says and be overwhelmed with adrenaline, which is what powers our fight/flight response. The lizard part of our brains is usually in charge at that point. None of the protocols, except the Check Out protocol, is appropriate if you don't have the full functionality of your thoughts and feelings. So, if you are going to interact with someone about intent or anything else, wait until adrenaline has cleared your system. Exercise, especially anything that gets your blood pumping hard, helps you do that. When you feel calm and rational, return to the team and connect again.

The Intention Check protocol also works on yourself. You may not be on an adrenaline rush, but you may have lots of other reasons to check your own intent before confronting anyone about anything. Really ask yourself what outcome you want from your interaction. If your intent is to "fix" them, accuse them, hurt them, or shame them, Check Out and resolve to find your own intent first. Using a protocol to snooker someone is a terrible form of manipulation and doubly violates the Core Commitments.

Especially, don't do a drive-by intention check. A drive-by is dropping the phrase, "Intention Check," in the middle of a conversation without the intent to actually hear the other person's story. It sounds more like an accusation than a question, and if the person accused begins to explain her intent, the accuser typically doesn't pay attention but changes the subject, his deed done.

Chapter 7:

Get Unanimous Decisions:

Decider and Resolution

"Informed decision-making comes from a long tradition of guessing and then blaming others for inadequate results."

Scott Adams

Feeding the Monster

You're in a meeting with twelve other people. The implicit agenda is, "We have to figure out what to do about this project." The monster is already at work. It is especially fond of large-group discussion, and people who talk more than listen.

It doesn't take long before action is stalled. Team members are tired and hungry, and their butts are numb from the meeting room chairs. Half the team is backbiting and playing turf wars, and the other half is mentally off playing golf.

Lucy, the project manager, keeps trying to teach the team consensus-building and brainstorming techniques. This merely irritates the team members by taking up time they already believe they don't have. Lucy is getting more and more brittle, defensive, and self-conscious, as well as less effective. The less effective she becomes, the more control she tries to take. The breath of the monster is hot on her cheek.

Team members start leaving the room, and the ones still there are getting sarcastic and argumentative, or they have opened their laptops and are writing emails. After four hours, not a single decision has been made, and everyone still has his or her day job to finish. The team agrees to a plan no one likes, but is at least a ticket out of the meeting room. In the hallway as they head back to their desks, team members form groups of two and three to figure out how to avoid taking action on the decision, one they know is a really dumb idea.

The monster grins, and continues to whisper.

How Great Teams Create Time

Teams that create time never, ever agree to a decision, good or bad, and then actively sabotage it. Tacit public agreement followed by sabotage is worse than no agreement at all. The lack of integrity of these moments permeates a team, like ink in water, so that no one can trust his or her teammates to be honest in public. Eventually, no one can trust any agreement at all. And the time wasted by highly valuable and skilled people in large group decision-making getting nothing accomplished for hour after hour is staggering.

Teams create time by never trying to make decisions in large groups. And if a decision must be made, they seek unanimity in small groups, explicitly. Yes, unanimity.

If someone believes action must be taken, he or she is accountable to propose that action. If that proposal doesn't receive unanimous support by the team members present at the time, it is improved or dropped. Willingness to drop a proposal the team is lukewarm about undertaking is a key characteristic of a great team. It allows space for new and better ideas to be raised.

A lukewarm response is different from clear opposition to a proposal. Sometimes one or two people on a team will have a clear objection to a proposal. Any individual willing to stop the action of an entire team by voting down a proposal without a clear alternative is in danger of carrying the monster into the team space. A team of people in conversation, even a small one, uses a lot of time. Any behavior that stands in the way of completing the conversation and taking action must be well thought out.

So to keep the team in action, a team member will only counter a proposal if he or she has a better idea or simply cannot support the idea under any circumstances ("loss of life will surely follow" could be one reason to vote against a proposal). In fact, teams that know how to create time tend to support and improve, rather than stop a proposal altogether.

The most dangerous invitation to the monster is the free-for-all that ensues when one person has an objection, and everyone present feels the need to comment. On a great team, if someone has a better idea than what's proposed, only that person and the person proposing the solution need to discuss it. And everyone else who either supports it or loves the idea keeps his or her mouth shut. We don't need to hear everyone's supporting statements at this point. We simply need to make a decision and move forward into action.

The Core Commitment of having a bias toward action guides this tool explicitly.

The Core Protocols

Decider

Use the Decider protocol anytime you want to move a group immediately and unanimously towards results.

Steps

1. Proposer says, "I propose [concise, actionable behavior]."
2. Proposer says, "One, two, three."
3. Voters, using either Yes (thumbs up), No (thumbs down), or Support It (flat hand), vote simultaneously.
4. Voters who absolutely cannot get in on the proposal declare themselves by saying, "I am an absolute no. I won't get in." If this occurs, the proposal is withdrawn.
5. Proposer counts the votes.
6. Proposer withdraws the proposal if a combination of outliers (No votes) and Support It votes is too great, or if Proposer expects not to successfully conclude the Resolution protocol (below). You can approximate "too great" by using the following heuristics:

i. approximately 50 percent (or greater) of votes are Support It, or
ii. the anticipated gain if the proposal passes is less than the likely cost of the resolution effort

7. Proposer uses the Resolution protocol with each outlier to bring him in by asking, "What will it take to get you in?"
8. Proposer declares the proposal carried if all outliers change their votes to Yes or Support It.
9. The team is now committed to the proposed result.

COMMITMENTS

- Propose no more than one item per proposal.
- Remain present until the Decider protocol is complete; always remain aware of how your behavior either moves the group forward or slows it down.
- Give your full attention to a proposal over and above all other activity.
- Speak only when you are the Proposer or are directed to speak by the Proposer.
- Keep the reasons you voted as you did to yourself during the protocol.
- Reveal immediately when you are an absolute No voter and be ready to propose a better idea.
- Be personally accountable for achieving the results of a Decider commitment even if it was made in your absence.

- Keep informed about Decider commitments made in your absence.
- Do not argue with an absolute No voter. Always ask him or her for a better idea.
- Actively support the decisions reached.
- Use your capacity to "stop the show" by declaring you "won't get in no matter what" with great discretion and as infrequently as possible.
- Insist at all times that the Decider and Resolution protocols be followed exactly as per specification, regardless of how many times you find yourself doing the insisting.
- Do not pass during the Decider protocol.
- Unceasingly work toward forward momentum; have a bias toward action.
- Do not look at how others are voting to choose your own vote.
- Avoid using the Decider protocol in large groups. Break up into small subgroups to make decisions, and use the large group to report status.

Notes

- Vote No only when you really believe the contribution to forward momentum you will make to the group, after slowing or stopping it in the current vote, will greatly outweigh the (usually considerable) costs you are adding by voting No.
- If you are unsure or confused by a proposal, vote Support It and seek clarification offline

after the proposal is resolved. If you have an alternate proposal after receiving more information, you can have faith that your team will support the best idea. (See the Core Commitments.)

- Voting No to make minor improvements to an otherwise acceptable proposal slows momentum and should be avoided. Instead, offer an additional proposal after the current one passes or, better yet, involve yourself in the implementation to make sure your idea gets in.
- Withdraw weak proposals. If a proposal receives less than 70 percent (approximately) Yes votes, it is a weak proposal and should be withdrawn by Proposer. This decision is, however, at the discretion of Proposer.
- Think of yourself as a potential solo outlier every time you vote No.
- Vote Absolute No only when you are convinced you have a significant contribution to make to the direction or leadership of the group, or when integrity absolutely requires it of you.

RESOLUTION

When the Decider protocol yields a small minority of outliers, the Proposer quickly leads the team, in a highly structured fashion, to deal with the outliers. The Resolution protocol promotes forward momentum by focusing on bringing outliers in at the least cost.

STEPS

1. Proposer asks outlier, "What will it take to get you in?"
2. Outlier states in a single, short, declarative sentence the precise modification required to be in.
3. Proposer offers to adopt the outlier's changes or withdraws the proposal.

NOTES

- If the outlier's changes are simple, a simple eye-check is performed to determine if everyone is still in.
- If the outlier's changes are complex, Proposer must withdraw the current proposal and submit a new proposal that incorporates the outlier's changes.
- If the outlier begins to say why he voted No or to explain anything other than what it will take to get him in, Proposer must interrupt the outlier with "What will it take to get you in?"

CREATE TIME YOURSELF

If you have a reasonable team to work with, you can simply introduce the protocol and suggest you all try it for a while as written to see what happens. Give yourselves time to get the rules straight. Just like learning to play a new card game, it's helpful to have the rules handy while you're trying it out.

If you are on a team that needs to be warmed up to the idea, try the following small steps. At the next meeting you're in, try focusing your own thinking on the purpose of the meeting. It's possible there is a decision required, but it's also possible the meeting is for a status update, information transfer, or some other reason. Be aware of the specific reason you are giving up time to be in the room.

When you have filtered the threads of the conversation to one or two ideas, look for proposals of action. If there is a decision to be made, ask explicitly, "Does anyone have a proposal?" Or if people are sharing ideas, and the conversation has settled on one or two, choose the idea you personally would be willing to work on and state, "I propose [current idea]. Who supports it? Does anyone oppose it?"

If there is disagreement, ask the outlier to share what it will take for him to agree. If others start commenting on your conversation, explicitly ignore them and stay focused on the person in opposition. If he can't offer an improvement to the idea, and the rest of the team supports it, suggest moving forward with the proposal for now until a better idea comes along. And share with him that it's in no one's interests to agree publicly and then undermine the agreement privately. When he has a better idea, he can propose it.

If the rest of the team is lukewarm on the proposal, it's probably best to drop it altogether. Another great idea will come along any minute.

Sometimes a team can get past the stalled point, but if the team gets stuck in ruminating over an idea without a decision to act, break up the meeting and do something else for a while. If the team repeatedly stalls in making decisions, look for other monster-feeding behaviors. The monster is in the room with you and is getting stronger and fatter with every meeting.

Chapter 8:

Give and Get Only Value: Perfection Game

"Criticism comes easier than craftsmanship."

Zeuxis

Feeding the Monster

The website has to be launched in two days. Larry was assigned to the task of creating it, and he's been working fourteen hours a day for three weeks, weekends included (on overtime), to get it done.

Gretta, the boss, is nervous. Larry's a great guy—very nice, quiet, and earnest—but he lacks experience with design, and when she asked if anyone had seen the site yet, they all shook their heads.

Gretta decides she's going to ask to see the site. "But it's not ready," Larry says, and goes pale. Gretta insists, and when Larry shows it to her, she feels ill. It's technically functional, and has all the features they require, but it's ugly. Butt ugly.

"What happened to the design?" Gretta asks.

Larry looks sheepish. "I asked the guys on the team to have a look at the site," he says. "And they told me all the things they didn't like. They pretty much tore it to shreds. So I thought I'd better take out all the stuff they didn't like."

"That's it? They didn't give you alternatives? Other ideas?" Gretta asks, incredulous.

"Every time we talked about it, the meeting would be over by the time they were finished telling me what they didn't like, and there was no time left to talk about what they wanted instead," Larry says.

Gretta realizes she's going to have to put off the launch, announce the delay to the investors, and bring new resources onto the team. She cancels her weekend plans and calls the team together for an emergency meeting. They're all going to be working overtime now.

The monster smirks, shifts its massive bulk and settles again.

When we are criticized or corrected, or a mistake is raised, we stop. It's natural, probably evolutionary. On the wrong path to hunt your next meal? Stop and return to safety. Entering enemy territory? Stop and regroup. Even if our actions won't lead to life or death, the monster would have you believe they will. We feel the shame or judgment of having been wrong, and we stop. It takes time to apply energy and force to get back into motion, if we ever do.

And unless we are extraordinarily centered, when we start again we might be slower to act, more timid, and more self-conscious, or we might just go the other way, becoming recklessly oppositional. Whatever our response, we've wasted time not just while stopped, but perhaps for a long period afterward.

How Great Teams Create Time

The Ask For Help protocol is the most important protocol to learn. It underlies all the others, as you've seen with the other protocols. On a team where asking for help is "just what we do," the Investigate protocol is a way to get the ideas out of our own heads. Someone asks us questions that make us think and find answers.

There's another opportunity, of course, which is asking for the ideas that are in other people's heads. Asking others for ideas and improvement, early and often, is second nature on a team that can create time. Team members using all the protocols and Core Commitments can continually provide new, insightful, innovative value about how to make the product great in the course of working on it.

Creating time happens when we ask for new ideas and new value, as often as possible and from as many people as will offer them. The monster would like us to think that all that asking will slow us down. But no matter how many ideas they've already received, or how great the product already is, teams that create time and are free of the monster keep asking. They ask within the team, and outside it. They ask people who have no idea what the product is about, and people who are intimately familiar with it.

A little better, a bit more, or a tiny improvement isn't enough. In offering value, they go for it, offering crazy ideas and blow-'em-away value. They imagine things that haven't been invented yet. They offer suggestions from their wildest dreams.

They leave "How to make it happen" to the next step. And if the person asking for the value can use even one of the ideas offered, they know the asking was worth it. These teams also allow the person asking for value to retain the right to do nothing with it. To these teams, ideas are a dime a dozen, and there's no cost to sharing them.

They also don't waste any time on "I don't like," "That sucks," and "You aren't serious." Negative statements put the brakes on action and don't sell more products. Every single idea gets put on the table and seriously considered. They get really present to the work in question and figure out what would make it spectacularly good. Impossible to resist. Magnificent.

THE CORE PROTOCOL

Perfection Game

The Perfection Game protocol will support you in your desire to aggregate the best ideas. Use it whenever you desire to improve something you've created.

STEPS

1. Perfectee performs an act or presents an object for perfection, optionally saying, "Begin" and "End" to notify the Perfector of the start and end of the performance.

2. Perfector rates the value of the performance or object on a scale of one to ten, based on how much value the Perfector believes he or she can add.
3. Perfector says, "What I liked about the performance or object was X," and proceeds to list the qualities of the object the Perfector thought were of high quality or should be amplified.
4. Perfector offers the improvements to the performance or object required for it to be rated a ten by saying, "To make it a ten, you would have to do X."

COMMITMENTS

- Accept perfecting without argument.
- Give only positive comments, such as what you like and what it would take to "give it a ten."
- Abstain from mentioning what you don't like or being negative in other ways.
- Withhold points only if you can think of improvements.
- Use ratings that reflect a scale of improvement rather than a scale of how much you liked the object.
- If you cannot say something you liked about the object or specifically say how to make the object better, you must give it a ten.

NOTES

- A rating of ten means you are unable to add value, and a rating of five means you will specifically describe how to make the object at least twice as good.
- The important information to transmit in the Perfection Game protocol improves the performance or object. For example, you could say, "The ideal sound of a finger snap for me is one that is crisp, has sufficient volume, and startles me somewhat. To get a ten, you would have to increase your crispness."
- As Perfectee, you may only ask questions to clarify or gather more information for improvement. If you disagree with the ideas given to you, simply don't include them.

CREATE TIME YOURSELF

If someone asks you for feedback, ideas, or opinions, offer the format of the Perfection Game protocol.

Say, "What I like is X, Y, and Z, so keep those things. What would make it absolutely amazingly perfect for me is A, B, C, and D."

Stay away from "I don't like..." Period.

Since we've all been raised to put energy into criticism and correction, most people find not being able to say what they don't like very difficult. It's rare to go a day without hearing or reading a personal opinion stated in the negative "for your own good."

We live in a world of criticism so ubiquitous that suggesting we shouldn't give feedback or tell someone what we don't like is akin to saying we shouldn't drive or use a telephone. Though there are lots of people who don't have a car and find alternatives to using a phone, for the majority of us, it would take an act of conscious effort to make the shift. For some, it takes a similar effort to offer only what we like and the value we can add. Do it anyway.

If you can't think of what would be an improvement, give it a ten, and let it go.

If you absolutely can't stop thinking about what you don't like and have to say something, be formulaic in stating your value. Try to turn what you don't like 180 degrees in your own mind. For instance, if the thought in your head is, "I don't like the font you've used," then consider what font you would like. Figure that out and say, "To make it a ten, you'd use a twelve-point sans serif bold font."

Finally, make sure you take it as well as you dish it out. Ask others to perfect something of yours. Show them the format of the protocol, or just tell them (it's pretty simple). If they stray into "I don't like," just say, "What would you like to see?" Then without arguing or defending, thank them for the value they've offered. And ask the next person on your list.

The Perfection Game protocol is particularly useful for getting ideas on products in development. It's also a lot of fun with kids and spouses.

Chapter 9:

Light A Fire: Scary Idea

"Here's to the crazy ones, the misfits, the rebels, the troublemakers, the round pegs in the square holes... the ones who see things differently -- they're not fond of rules... You can quote them, disagree with them, glorify or vilify them, but the only thing you can't do is ignore them because they change things... they push the human race forward, and while some may see them as the crazy ones, we see genius, because the ones who are crazy enough to think that they can change the world, are the ones who do."

Steve Jobs

Feeding the Monster

The same old ideas rehashed over and over. And over. Invested in, worked on, repaired, fixed, improved, tweaked, and tolerated.

You know how it works. You've been in those facilitated brainstorming meetings. You're told the rules, and you know very well no one will take them or the ideas seriously. Despite even the best facilitators and their methods, anything new and innovative is shot down as "off topic," "unrealistic," or worse "blue sky," if not in the meeting then afterward in the hallways and cubicles.

The monster invented the phrase "That'll never work." Repressing all ideas blocks great ideas from ever seeing the light of day. "Didya hear what the new kid came up with the other day? That might have flown where he used to work, but he's gotta realize this place is different. It's just not how we do things around here."

The beast also shows up in the assumption that what didn't work for us before, won't work for us now. "Don't say those things in front of the boss. He shot down a project just like that last year. And the guy who proposed it is gone now." Yet, how many other things have changed in the intervening time? This could be just the idea the boss is waiting for. And you won't know until you try it. But because the time-eating monster talks to us constantly to keep us fearful of losing safety and control, ideas that could save the company from being beaten by its competitors remain carefully locked up inside heads, and the monster's voice provides an endless stream of reasons for that to continue. "People will say it's crazy, or too complicated. We don't know how to do it. We've never done anything that big before. That's not our core competence. It's not on the CEO's Top Ten List. We don't have the budget. We don't have enough people to make it happen."

What those thoughts really mean is it's just too scary to think of doing something that great.

We take the safe route, the controlled route, the one we usually take, or the one our competitors have taken. We work toward a predictable, well-thought-out idea and move into production with it. Safety and predictability are for payroll and taxes, not for world-changing ideas, complex problems, and innovation.

How Great Teams Create Time

Members of Great teams passionately share their wildest ideas with each other. To do that, they share all their new ideas without judgment, delay, competition, or expectation of reward or ownership.

Great teams also separate idea-sharing from decision-making. The hardest part for everyone, even on a great team, is getting the scary idea into fresh air, getting it out of one startled and awed head and into many. Ideas get to live and breathe for a while, long enough to be improved or replaced by a better idea, not by one that's safe and easily planned and controlled.

Then, if a team is passionate enough about making it happen, someone will propose a course of action, and through a unanimous decision the whole team takes action and remains committed to its execution until a better idea comes along. It's as simple as that. The team uses all the protocols at its disposal, perfects the idea, moves into action, prototypes, perfects again, shares again, and iterates.

Some ideas die a natural death. Some are out of scope within our current capability. Others take on a life of their own, enriched by a serendipitous new and concurrent technology, culture change, business direction, economic upheaval, or simple change in the team. Some make the organization wildly successful. But we will never know if team members don't say them out loud.

Members of great teams commit to share their fearsome ideas out loud and without judgment, with people who have different perspectives, experiences, and ways of thinking and talking about ideas. Only writing them down doesn't cut it. Few ideas are as inspiring in an email or proposal as they are when expressed by a human voice. And the goal is simply to say it.

THE CORE PROTOCOL

Scary Idea

Use the Scary Idea protocol to ensure that you have exhausted your creative resources. Mostly, people don't say their ideas because of some type of fear. Use the Scary Idea protocol to acknowledge your fear and move forward.

STEPS

1. Say, "I have a scary idea" and state and/or show your idea.

OR

2. Ask the group, "Has everyone expressed her scariest ideas?"

NOTES

- ☐ Use the Decider protocol to convert the ideas into action(s).
- ☐ Use the Perfection Game protocol to add value to the idea.
- ☐ If you feel you want your or another's idea to be even greater, repeat the Scary Idea protocol.

More on the Scary Idea Protocol

When we say, "Scary," we don't mean scary as in a horror movie or frightening ghost story. We mean that if your idea is scary, it will most likely require courage to state it. If courage is wisdom while feeling fear, then you would have to ask yourself if your idea is wise (if it will get others to think bigger or more creatively) and then decide to express your idea in spite of your fear. People are scared to say their ideas for many different reasons, and the most common reason is the fear of being ostracized, laughed at, rejected, or not accepted by their peers.

Whatever your reason for holding back a scary or big idea, consider that each time you choose not to share these ideas, you are limiting your team's potential. Even if your idea is unusual or impossible to realize, someone on your team may be able to think of ways to make some version of it realized, or at least it will inspire them to think of a better one. The point is, get your ideas out—especially the scary ones.

CREATE TIME YOURSELF

Deliberately, randomly, and regularly ask team members to share their scariest ideas. Ask them about the ones that set their guts on fire, the ones that they have no idea how to execute, but that they would work on in their pajamas in their spare time if they could. Ask them if they didn't have to figure out how to make it happen, what would they want the product or service to do, provide, or create.

Don't use facilitators, meeting leaders, or timekeepers. Don't manage the meeting. Don't have an agenda.

Don't have a process. Just say ideas. Out loud. When you're on the right track you'll giggle uncomfortably and want to be more practical. Don't. You'll hear words like, "Wow" and "Whoa" and, I hope, other words you wouldn't normally use. Let it go and enjoy. It will be tempting to stop the ideas from coming because the possibility of greatness is temporarily uncomfortable. Don't be "sensible." Don't "stay on topic." You have lots of time to do that later. Maximize the ratio of scary ideas to practical ones. I guarantee that you will never, ever think of too many.

Use the word "pretend." A lot. "Pretend we had the technology [or money, staff, skills, partners] to make this crazy idea happen. What then?"

For every scary idea on the table, ask the team to try to top it. You'll know you're using the protocol correctly when the whole team stares in delighted disbelief at each other, pondering the implications of a world with this idea in it.

Chapter 10:

Go First

Protocol Check

"We promise according to our hopes, and perform according to our fears."

Francois duc de la Rochefoucauld

Feeding the Monster

The monstrous voice whispers phrases like these in our ears: "He's not following the rules. That's dragging the rest of the team down. And he just won't listen so why should I bother trying myself?"

"How can I work in this place where no one else is as committed as I am? I give up."

"People just don't want to be great. It's pointless to even try."

We are social animals and take our cues from one another. We also unconsciously measure the cost of change and keep doing what we've always done, until doing something different is less costly than maintaining the status quo.

The combination of these two behaviors is murder if the team wants to change how it works together. We watch, evaluate, and watch some more. "Is anyone else putting her neck out to say the obvious? To tell him he's breaking the rules? No? Well then, I won't either. Why should I? And besides, there's no real reason to push it. Things aren't that bad."

It is rare to see one person voluntarily break the status quo and compassionately, respectfully note a broken promise or missed deadline. When that happens, however, we've created time.

How Great Teams Create Time

Everyone is accountable for quality, always. It never stops, goes away, slows down, or becomes less important. Once there is a high level of trust and commitment, the only way to maintain that state is to remain as rigorous about accountability as when you started. And in fact, it does become easier over time. Once you've seen and felt a high-trust environment, you'll never want to go back. Another person bringing your attention to a mistake is much less painful than systemic suspicion and sabotage. And we will make mistakes, so it's time to learn how to deal with it.

We're all human, after all. We lose the plot, forget, revert to old behaviors, and get distracted. And if we're aligned within ourselves, committed to a sensible, common set of rules and tools, and supported by people we trust, a compassionate and respectful pause in the action to catch those moments is no big deal. If promises aren't met, timelines are missed or about to be, or commitments are broken, every person must take the responsibility to call the play, to reset the level of quality to where the team needs it to be to continue to create time.

Quality starts with the Core Commitments. Being personally willing to check not just one's own level of commitment, but that of others is the only way to keep quality high. It's called shared leadership. Having a great idea, catching quality issues, making decisions, and providing value are activities every team member on every kind of team can learn.

On a great team, there are no parents, authority figures, or police to make people do what must be done. The team has everything it needs, including simple tools to use in circumstances like this. And that means there's no reason to wait for someone else with more skills, charisma, training, or some other excuse to fix the problem. The team must fix it now, before the monster gets its toehold. Because if we wait for someone else to catch it and fix it when it happens, time slips out of our grasp. The monster will make sure of it. The monster slips through the cat door of a team the moment we tolerate a broken promise or little white lie.

On a great team everyone is willing and able and ready to go first.

THE CORE PROTOCOL

Protocol Check

Use the Protocol Check when you believe a protocol is being used incorrectly in any way or when a Core Commitment is being broken.

STEPS

1. Say, "Protocol Check."
2. If you know the correct use of the protocol, state it. If you don't, Ask For Help.

COMMITMENTS

- Say, "Protocol Check" as soon as you become aware of the incorrect use of a protocol, or of a broken Core Commitment. Do this regardless of the current activity.
- Be supportive of anyone using Protocol Check.
- Do not shame or punish anyone using Protocol Check.
- Ask For Help as soon as you realize you are unsure of the correct protocol use.

CREATE TIME YOURSELF

You go first.

Be the one to call it out. Far from feedback, this is a formal, simple comparison of intent against execution: "I noticed you did Y. We had agreed to X." Be the one to represent the integrity of the team. It's uncomfortable to be the one calling it out. We got beaten up for doing that in school, and we still remember it. But we're not in school any more. Doing an uncomfortable thing now will reap magnificent rewards in future.

Being willing to check quality peacefully, with compassion, and without judgment or competition is one of the purest forms of leadership. Check your intent, and remember your Personal Alignment protocol. Focusing on the virtue or quality you are working on can help put you in the right mindset for this task. Also, remember that most people act with the best intent. They genuinely want to work well with others.

Finally, ask others to help you. Don't allow yourself to become the policeman for the team. Whether you do it, or the boss or facilitator does it, expecting only one person to have responsibility for quality invites the monster to take over. If every person agreed to follow the protocols, then everyone should be equally committed to supporting and using them.

Chapter 11:

Be a Great Boss

"For me, this is a familiar image - people in the organization ready and willing to do good work, wanting to contribute their ideas, ready to take responsibility, and leaders holding them back, insisting that they wait for decisions or instructions."

Margaret J. Wheatley

Feeding the Monster

The team has been working on a complex product for months. They have missed three milestones in the last two weeks. When they do meet their deadlines, the results are never quite complete or satisfying. Quality and completeness are always at a frustrating 90 percent. The team energy is dropping, and the lower the energy gets the more they lose timeliness and quality. The team complains there are too many tasks to be completed in the time available, and they are overwhelmed.

Their boss, Bill, starts getting worried. The monster is ever-present for him, nagging him to intervene. He knows from experience that when he steps in, the team gets less done, not more, but this time things are really serious. Or at least, so the voice says. Bill decides something needs to be done. He brings in more staff, hires an extra project manager, and joins their status meetings weekly. He asks to see the status reports and to be updated daily.

When Bill goes to the meetings, he can tell there's something wrong, but he's not sure what. The monster has been working on them too, advising them to keep the real truth from anyone who has the power to hire and fire, and to put some pressure on the managers to fix the symptoms. In the meetings, he notices the team members fight about who's going to do what, how their workspace is laid out, how often they have to update the project manager, and how confusing the project plan is. Bill is reminded of his own peer-management team and its meetings. He vows he'll find a solution before this team gets as dysfunctional as his.

The next milestone they deliver is even further behind. A team member asks Bill if he can speak privately, and he shares some serious concerns about Andy and Rachel who, the team member says, are continually asking stupid questions and slowing the team down. If those two weren't on the team, he says, the team could forge ahead. Bill says he'll look into it. The project-management meetings begin to sound like family feuds.

Bill has to start spending his evenings in his home office, catching up on the rest of his work. He misses his daughter's school play, and he forgets his anniversary. His wife and kids have started ignoring him at home; no wonder, he thinks, since he's rarely there.

Bill's boss starts asking skill-testing questions about the troubled project. Apparently, there have been complaints from some of Bill's peers on the management team that Bill isn't pulling his weight for all the resources he's using, and they are wondering about his ability to handle the staff load he has. The implication is he'd better get it together, and soon.

How Great Bosses Create Time

Great bosses are consistently clear about what they want and rational about timeliness and results. They represent the symbolic or real authority of the paying customer, the owner of the final product.

A great boss expects the team to produce results. All a great boss cares about is that the results are on time and great. That's it. If the results aren't great and on time, there's a problem on the team, and the boss expects the team to solve that problem, including asking the boss for help if necessary, but never expecting the boss to be on the team or do the team's work. Payment for results is the exchange between a boss and a team. Team members have each other for help, and they have the simple rules and tools to stay in action, make decisions, communicate, and deliver.

A great boss doesn't care about or interfere in how the team gets results. The team's skills and ability to figure that out is why the boss hired them and why they get paid. The boss expects the team to use each other to solve the problem of how to get results. If the team isn't doing that, there's a problem on the team that the team, not the boss, needs to deal with.

Being a boss is not about leadership of employees. Leadership occurs on a team of peers. A leader is one who has an idea and does what is necessary, including seeking the help of others, to move it productively into reality. That's what bosses hire employees to do.

When bosses start doing employees' jobs, especially if they interfere with solving team problems, the monster slithers into existence.

For instance, if a team member doesn't get a key product finished, or the quality of the result is too low to meet the standard expected by the customers, the team is not taking responsibility for the overall quality of the result. A great team will deal with that problem itself, before it becomes the boss's problem. And the boss won't give in to his or her own ego in wanting to be the hero and fix the problem.

It's only when there is the clear potential for unplanned loss of revenue, reputation, or customers, or there is potential for loss of life or legal action, that the boss might step in and take action. That intervention should be very specific. It is to remind the team of its responsibilities and to be clear about the impact the problem is having on overall results. Then the team needs to fix the problems that allowed the product to be missed in the first place. And the boss needs to examine how the team became so dysfunctional in the first place, first looking to him or herself for the root of the problem. We usually find the behavior of the team can be traced to the same behavior in the boss. That's an example of Team = Product.

The problem on the team can come from one or more missed Core Commitments. Team members agree to hold each other accountable for keeping commitments, and to remain interested in the quality and timeliness of the total product, not just their own piece of it. If a team member won't accept or use help from other team members, for instance, it affects the overall results of the whole team, which is something everyone should be concerned about.

For instance, a team member may feel personal ownership for part of a product and consciously or unconsciously avoid using the team to get help, in order to be recognized individually. I think of this as the Hero Problem. The boss can unconsciously contribute to this behavior by rewarding individual work rather than the final overall result.

The Hero Problem can show up as defensiveness or isolation, and in appeals to the boss for personal attention. Here, leadership on the team can become confused with ownership. Leading action on a part of the product that is important to the final result is very positive. A great team member will move action forward on product development by using all the team resources available, including help, perfection, and ideas from the other members of the team.

But it's important to separate ownership from responsibility. The team neither owns the product nor any piece of the product. They own the experience of creation, not what is created. The owner of the product is whoever is paying for it to be created. The team members are responsible to stay focused on the overall results, and to use resources effectively to achieve the goals of the product owner. Bosses help the team stay focused by representing the customer to the employee team.

Bosses sometimes forget that they are on a team themselves. The team the boss is on is usually some kind of management team of peers. The management team's product is the employee team. If the employee teams are humming, productive, happy, and delivering great products on time every time, the management team has produced a great product. On their own team, bosses are team members, responsible to produce a product, an aligned productive organization, and ask each other for help. With their employee team, he or she is a boss, expecting great results on time on behalf of a customer.

When working on their own team, the bosses have a responsibility to use each other to perfect, get ideas, solve problems, and support each other. Yet, management teams are just as vulnerable to the monster as are employee teams. Fortunately, the solutions are exactly the same, because regardless of the product being created, the patterns that work and don't work on teams are universal.

Entrepreneurs are a special case. The boss often continues to participate on the employee team creating products. The unique case of a boss being a team contributor as well requires more clarity about what role is in play in any conversation.

In this case, however, the individual playing both roles explicitly acknowledges the different roles he plays. "This is a boss moment" is a great way to start a conversation about timeliness or quality. "Boss moments" imply non-negotiable direction or requests, including either a delivery date for the product, or the high-level specifications for that product, but not both. Then, saying, "As a team contributor I have an idea," is a way to shift back into a team-member role and make it clear that the idea must be evaluated for merit with all other ideas.

The very best bosses are exemplary models of dedicated use of the most efficient simple rules and tools. Most have learned the hard way that the only way to get their work done and still enjoy health and their families, and reach their personal goals, is by creating time.

Chapter 12:

Take It Home

"The instruction we find in books is like fire. We fetch it from our neighbours, kindle it at home, communicate it to others, and it becomes the property of all."

Voltaire

Way back at the beginning of the book we talked about how we can't separate ourselves into little compartments, one for work and another for everything else. Similarly, we can't separate home from everything else. The common thread across your work, home, and everywhere else is you. You carry all your experiences, skills, behaviors, and desires everywhere you go.

Once you've tried the simple rules and tools and had some success, you'll be inspired to use them everywhere. Just like you, we've been excited to share the tools with others. As we worked with people and shared the tools, we saw that, just like getting a new computer, phone, or app, the temptation is to tell people, "I've found this really cool tool, it's exactly what *you* need!"

Avoid that temptation at all costs. It doesn't work. Not only does it not work, you might find you're not invited to people's parties any more.

What people are attracted to, however, is a great example. Think of your teachers, mentors, neighbours, and others, who have inspired you because they "walked the talk," or, more practically, they were models of the message they brought to others.

So rather than pulling out the "do as I say" card, do yourself what you believe must be done. You might get some strange looks, some cynicism, maybe even some resistance. Don't let that stop you. Your integrity over time will be the example that makes it possible for others to consider trying the tools themselves, and see that they work. And if no one else chooses to try them, use them yourself anyway.

If you want to try some of the tools at home, we've found that kids and partners love to Check In and Check Out.

Checking Out during a fight will stop the cycle of winning-at-all-costs and give you time to physically recover from the adrenaline rush of the argument. You can then come back refreshed and ready to reconnect.

Again, modeling helps everyone. One person's courage to Check Out makes it clear it's a tool available to everyone else, so model it early in a low-tension moment, such as during a movie or a family gathering that isn't interesting to you.

As a parent, Check Out can be your best friend. But be sure you have a responsible adult who will take your place with a child while you're Checked Out. And if children Check Out, be sure you know where they are and that they're safe. If your partner Checks Out, thank him or her for his or her courage and commitment to your relationship. Never, ever get mad at someone for Checking Out. If you do, you're breaking one of the Core Commitments, and you're taking the option away from yourself as well.

If you are still able to think straight, try Checking In and then Asking For Help with the reason for your emotions. If I Check In angry, I'll find the reason in myself and then ask Paul for help with it. He's usually relieved the cause wasn't him! And that reminds me, never ever Check In blaming another person for your feelings. Find the cause in yourself. For instance, let's say the kids promised to do the laundry and didn't. Now you don't have a shirt for tomorrow's board meeting.

Find the cause in yourself. Did you specifically ask them to do it today? Did you give them a timeline? Were you absolutely clear, or could they have misinterpreted your instructions? Have you missed any commitments lately, creating a model in which missing commitments was okay with you? Have you missed any commitments to them?

And then, ultimately, the important question is, "What's going to be different next time?" Have that discussion now.

In fact, institute a statute of limitations on Checking In about broken commitments, missed promises, or bad behavior. In our house, it's three days. After that, the incident goes in the circular file. That avoids the conversations that go like this: "You didn't pick up your socks, again. In fact you haven't picked up your socks since 1973, and I'm really mad."

That's just not a conversation an adult should be having. If not picking up socks is something that needs to change, ask for it the first time it happens. If it's been twenty-eight years of sock clutter, then you can't complain. You contributed to it by letting it go on without comment. And no, not everyone has the same expectations you have.

Start from scratch with the most recent sock episode, leave references to the past out of it, and ask for help by saying, "Will you pick up your socks?" and go from there, remembering that "No" is valid. Only when there has been an explicitly agreed commitment that has been broken can you ask the question, "We agreed you were going to pick up your socks. What happened? What's going to be different next time?"

Lots of parents Check In with their kids at bedtime. If you're going to do that, remember it's respectful, regardless of their age, to not question their Check In. But if people want to share the cause of their emotions, then that's a lovely opportunity for connection through the Investigate protocol.

Again, to model sharing the cause of emotions is the most successful approach. Instead of asking the child why they feel what they feel, model volunteering the cause of your own emotions, using language the child understands. Your willingness to be honest and share your feelings will help them grow and learn that emotions aren't bad, but that they're just there and will pass, and while we feel them, they help us connect with each other.

Asking your teenagers for help, especially with things you both enjoy, can balance out the power struggle during those years. Again, be rational, and don't sweat it if they say no. Building a family culture of the right to say yes or no, without shame or guilt, will go a long way toward world peace.

The Investigate protocol is particularly powerful for parents with teenagers. Teens are used to, and frequently become numb to, parents questioning with a transparent agenda: "Where were you last night?" or "You're not going out like that are you?" And like the rest of us, they resent unsolicited feedback: "You shouldn't hang out with that boy anymore. He's a bad influence."

Parents can also easily get caught up in drama. Just like the boss who jumps in to fix a problem for his or her team, parents want to fix their children's problems. But any parent who has tried that knows how painful the rebuttal can be. That's where the Investigate protocol can help a parent stay objective but remain connected, providing the child with a caring but non-judgmental home base as she figures out who she is in the world.

And just as we wish our own children would ask us for help, model that behavior by asking your own parents for help. You might be surprised how valuable it can be.

Afterword

"As human beings, our greatness lies not so much in being able to remake the world - that is the myth of the atomic age - as in being able to remake ourselves."
Mohandas Gandhi

The call to action

I believe we all can create time, and we must. We need teams to deal with the complexity of our world. Waiting for experts to feed us one small idea at a time is a reliable way to feed the monster. We need teams that are self-sufficient, efficient, and innovative. They can be technical teams, education teams, community groups, families, work teams, temporary and permanent teams, in-person and virtual teams, and more.

What we've learned is that every team will develop simple rules, whether implicit or explicit, tested or not. Those simple rules tell team members what the team boundaries are, and they give team members shortcuts for communicating.

The emergent approaches of self-organization, open-source software and knowledge, crowd sourcing through social media, and self-managed teams are becoming ubiquitous among the organizations that are actually recovering and thriving in the post-financial-collapse economy.

Every organization has found its own flavor of the universal set of simple rules and tools through trial and error. But trial and error takes a long time. We all need a way to self-organize quickly to solve the problems we have created for ourselves. And then we need to create the next world where we can thrive.

The simple rules and tools here are a subset of a rich and powerful set of team tools that have emerged from the evolution of teams in a lab. For teams using the homegrown equivalent of tin cans and a string for communication, these tools are the newest and most radically efficient technology for removing constraints and improving performance.

This work coincides with a recent growing discontent with the institutions of the twentieth century, including management science. The possibilities for sharing information freely, self-organizing around ideas, and building solutions without someone "in charge" are both consequences of, and adaptations to, our new world. We don't have time, nor should we have the patience, to wait while facilitators, experts and politicians lead us where they think we should go.

My call to action to you is to just use the tools. You know what needs to be done to make you life and the lives around you less painful and more magnificent. Because you know what has to be done, you're the best person to do it. Find the tool that you need right now to move forward and though it's difficult and uncomfortable and scary, use it. Use it over and over until that feeling of discomfort and awkwardness goes away. Like playing the piano or learning a game, one day you'll realize you aren't thinking about the what and how any more, you're thinking about the why and the what next.

I have not included all the protocols in this book, so I hope you will also explore the rest of the protocols and other material that makes up the Core System (www.liveingreatness.com) and the work of Jim and Michele McCarthy (www.mccarthyshow.com).

If you'd like to learn more about Human Systems Dynamics and the amazing work of the network of associates working in public, private and non-profit organizations around the world who are using and testing the science of self-organization in human systems, I encourage you to explore the work of Glenda Eoyang and the Human Systems Dynamics Institute (www.hsdinstitute.org).

To learn the tools of creating time, join us in a Creating Time BootCamp, which features the following:

- Five-day business game that gives people a taste of how to create time together using the rules and tools in a low-risk environment that is modeled on a real-world business project.
- Perfect opportunity to kick start a team into trust, shared vision, and high bandwidth communication.
- One-to-one coaching on demand during camp built into the game.
- Instructors adapting in the moment to the requirements of the team.

- Extensive manual containing everything we know about great teams and how to create them.
- Teams of all sizes, and individuals, welcome.
- Post-session advisory services available.

For more information, go to www.simplerulesandtools.com.

Notes From Human Systems Dynamics

For those of you who love science, this section is for you. As a relatively new student of Human Systems Dynamics (HSD), I will merely touch the surface of how I believe it underpins the Core System. The quotes I've included here are from the HSD Certification Training content, Cohort 15, held in Ottawa, Canada in the fall of 2010 and the PhD dissertation of Dr. Glenda Eoyang.

Human Systems Dynamics brings together hard sciences and organizational dynamics. HSD looks at human systems, like organizations, teams, communities, and groups, as complex adaptive self-organizing systems (CAS).

A CAS is a "collection of individual agents who have the freedom to act in unpredictable ways, and whose actions are interconnected such that they produce system-wide patterns." Patterns are "similarities, differences, and relationships that have meaning across space and/or time." (HSD Professional Certification Training, Cohort 15, Ottawa, Canada, Fall, 2010.)

Those system-wide patterns, in turn, influence the agents, creating dynamical change. This type of change happens when boundaries are open and agents are affected by influences that cannot be known or controlled, variables are co-dependent and none are primary, and there is no root cause in sight. Nonlinear causality is at play, and results are emergent rather than predictable and controlled.

Teams using the Core System have all of the characteristics of a CAS. They are free to act in whatever way they choose, and their actions are interdependent over space and time in ways that create patterns that individuals often cannot see all at once.

In addition, models and concepts from complexity science have been replicated in teams using the simple rules and tools. Patterns, particularly attractor patterns, are well managed by the Core System.

Dr. Glenda Eoyang's CDE Model of Human Systems

Intro

Dr. Glenda Eoyang's dissertation (CONDITIONS FOR SELF-ORGANIZING IN HUMAN SYSTEMS, Glenda Holladay Eoyang, The Union Institute and University, DECEMBER 28, 2001) introduced the elegant CDE model. This is from the introduction to that paper:

"The CDE Model posits three conditions that serve as meta-variables to shape the speed, path, and outcomes of self-organizing processes in human systems. The conditions of the CDE Model comprise:

- Container bounds the system of focus and constrains the probability of contact among agents;
- significant Difference establishes the potential for change within the system;
- transforming Exchange connects agents to each other through a transfer of information, energy, or material."

The CDE model, Eoyang's further research, and applications of the model in real human systems have provided me with a way of thinking about the Core System and why it is uniquely effective. Seeing the underlying rational scientific basis for the success of the Core System reinforces my commitment to using it on teams working on complex problems and prediction, like software development, poverty, environmental sciences, community action, and education reform.

Most interesting is the possibility of using knowledge about the three variables, and the tools of the Core System, to influence and shift the conditions to change patterns. Any one of container, difference, and exchange variables can be more or less constrained.

Containers can be made smaller or larger. On a team, that could mean breaking into pairs or subteams, or coming together as a large team. A Container can be more or less permeable; teams can include or exclude exchange with other teams and sources of difference. And Containers can be more or fewer; teams can increase or decrease the number of formally coupled subteams by separating or merging the subteams to achieve an optimal result.

In general, a more constrained variable makes the resulting pattern more organized, and a less constrained variable makes the resulting pattern less organized. Which to choose depends on the type of work that has to be done and the results that are desired.

Coupling also plays a part in choosing a response to the pattern. Tightly coupled exchanges and containers increase control and certainty. For instance, a micromanaging boss is tightly coupling his or her actions to those of the workers. Tightly coupled communication, like face-to-face meetings, requires a large time investment for a limited exchange of information. In this case, the clarity of communication and quality of the exchange must be extremely high, something the tools of the Core System optimizes. Tight couples are particularly important for emotional exchanges, and less important for status reporting, for instance.

Looser couples allow for growth and transformation. A boss who provides a clear expectation of requirements or timeliness, but expects employees to figure out the details of the work itself, allows the possibility of adaptation of the how, what, and when as appropriate. When the agents and their exchanges are completely uncoupled, results will be unpredictable. A boss who never interacts with his or her team will be too isolated to see patterns or influence results. Team members who rarely interact will never create patterns that can be influenced or lead to excellence.

As the agents interact with the system-wide patterns, the containers, differences, exchanges, coupling, and patterns will change.

CONTAINERS

A container represents boundaries in which agents interact and by which they are constrained.

In the "real world," containers are "multiple and massively entangled," (HSD Professional Certification Training, Cohort 15, Ottawa, Canada, Fall, 2010.) meaning it is impossible to isolate just one container that influences a team.

The Core System itself is a container. The Core Commitments bound the system of focus (the team) and optimally constrain the behaviours of the agents (team members). The Core Protocols bound the exchanges of difference within the team to only those that will result in high-value output.

There are nested layers of containers in which the Core System operates. The most basic container is a team member. The next layer is the team itself, and subsets of the team that emerge as work is done. The working team's manager is outside the team container he or she manages but is a member of a different team, a team of management peers, and his or her manager is in turn a member of a team. The organization is, therefore, a fractal of teams, with self-similarity at all levels of the organizational hierarchy. The organization and others like it, in turn, operate within containers of an economy, political entity (municipality, province, country), and environment.

Returning to the level of the team, one other container that influences the team is the size of the team. Significant difference—and therefore the possibility of innovation, adaptation, and growth—on the team is amplified with a larger number of team members and a large cognitive variety. For instance, a team of ten middle-class, English-speaking, North American JavaScript specialists may have less cognitive difference within the team container, and therefore a lower capacity to solve complex problems, than a team of ten people from different countries and classes with backgrounds in many areas of web development who all speak different languages.

In addition, the team laboratory of BootCamp is a container, "holding the agents together until system-wide patterns can emerge." (HSD Professional Certification Training, Cohort 15, Ottawa, Canada, Fall, 2010.) The far vision of the team is the container the team moves into after BootCamp.

By formalizing the use of only the most useful behaviors that can influence the system-wide patterns, and excluding the behaviors that will work against the team, the Core System reduces the signal-to-noise ratio and creates a perception of the creation of time. Since teams in organizations are fractal, with behaviors at all levels of the hierarchy influencing and amplifying patterns at all levels, the use of only the most successful behaviors reinforces and amplifies success throughout the dimensions of the organization.

DIFFERENCES (WITHIN AND BETWEEN)

Differences "provide the potential for change and define the emergent pattern." (HSD Professional Certification Training, Cohort 15, Ottawa, Canada, Fall, 2010.) HSD recognizes two aspects of difference: The variable to watch and the divergence in that variable at one time. For instance, the variable to watch may be leadership behavior. The divergence at any one time may give clues about whether there is enough or not enough leadership behavior.

Differences can be damped or amplified as required by the level of agreement and certainty the team must work in. Teams working in highly controlled, highly regulated organizations (taxation, manufacturing) may need to damp some difference in decision-making in the most routine of work to reduce the possibility of patterns changing too rapidly.

Teams working in emerging technologies, economics, or peacekeeping may need to amplify cognitive difference in order to generate enough possible solutions to the complex problems they face.

Within any team, there is divergence over time in emotions, physical energy and health, skills, wants, knowledge, and learning capacity. Within the team or between team members are cognitive, physical, cultural, and other differences. These are differences of experience, interest, values, health, skills, and more.

Importantly, the difference at one level of abstraction can be a container at another level. For instance, within an organization there can be many functional departments. The amount of difference between those departments helps define the patterns that will emerge overall. For instance, the difference between the goals and customer communications of the sales department and the service department can create a random pattern of customer expectations. At the department level, however, those differences disappear. The sales department's goals and customer communications are consistent within that department, and therefore become a container subject to influences of other differences.

The Core System optimizes difference within a team and between teams.

EXCHANGES

"Exchanges establish the connections among agents and between individuals and the whole." (HSD Professional Certification Training, Cohort 15, Ottawa, Canada, Fall, 2010.) Exchanges can be of anything: information, money, energy, ideas, or help. Transformational exchange is two-way, and may be formal or informal, and tightly or loosely coupled. The exchange can be used to amplify or damp a pattern, and encourage change or discourage it.

The Core Commitments provide simple rules for formalizing only the most useful aspects of the exchange in a team. Like flocking birds that stay not too close and not too far, avoid predators, and follow the lead bird, the simple rules for team members are in the form of Core Commitments.

Exchanges on the team include exchanges about emotions, ideas, decisions, wants, visions, products, services, and so on. One HSD associate noted that the Core Commitments and Core Protocols effectively reduce the signal-to-noise ratio in exchanges on the team, causing the perception of an increase in time. An increase in available time is a result of removing the activity noise we usually tolerate as a necessary evil in human systems.

HSD AND THE CORE SYSTEM

Using the HSD CDE model can help clarify the container, differences, and exchanges in play. Using the Core System then provides tools for how to respond to your clarified perspective.

Responses can include amplifying or damping conditions causing patterns, formalizing or making exchanges less formal, and making exchanges more or less tight. As Dr. Eoyang says, there are no right answers, and we can never know everything about a system, but we can become skilled at recognizing patterns and choosing a good response based on success in the past.

Using the Core System puts a team much farther ahead than if it had to start from scratch, learning the basic patterns of teams and the best ways to damp activity noise and amplify successful behaviors. In changing the patterns of the team, these three variables—container, differences, and exchanges—are necessary and sufficient. Change one, and the patterns in the system change.

Is the team in a pattern of getting stalled or stuck in groupthink in a large group? Not enough good ideas raised? One person talking and others listening all the time? A team member can take action to split up the container into smaller containers, such as subteams, tasks of shorter duration, more frequent milestones, or milestones with fewer features. This reduces the difference in the container, tightens the coupling between team members, and increases exchange bandwidth.

If a decision is stalled—that is, action is damped—splitting into subteams increases the bandwidth available for ideas to be exchanged and reduces differences to increase the likelihood of a decision being agreed upon. Using the Check In or Investigate protocols with each other on the subteams can shift exchanges from a high-divergence exchange to a low-divergence exchange.

If a team is shifting into "hero" mode—each contributor is isolating himself or herself and working alone—then it's not taking advantage of its greatest resource, which is internal cognitive diversity. One way to solve that problem is to deliberately increase the frequency or amplitude of exchanges of cognitive difference within the team through tools like the Scary Idea, Ask For Help or Perfection Game protocols. The exchange of feelings through Check In and Investigate also helps bridge the isolation gap.

Teams that are effectively using internal cognitive diversity, but are unsatisfied with the results, can increase divergence by changing the level of abstraction of the container and including more than just the current team members in ideation. Asking for help outside the team makes the container's boundaries more porous to ideas and increases divergence in exchanges. One simple way to amplify difference quickly is to ask for help from a group or person unfamiliar with the current team's work, or that works in a completely different domain. Software developers could ask for help from community services professionals. Teachers could ask for help from small business leaders. To be exceptionally effective, the group asked should be so far removed from the team's domain that there is no way to know what the help could be if it is offered.

A frequent challenge on teams is a core team being supplemented by new team members. The pattern that emerges is often voluntary isolation of the new and old teams from each other. From an HSD perspective, in this situation there are two containers with few exchanges of difference between them. To make the boundaries between the containers more permeable, and eventually to remove them altogether, the team with the thickest boundaries and highest resistance to change—the old team—must be the one to open up its container and cross the boundary. It can do this by explicitly seeking out the new team members, asking them for help, investigating their ideas, and deliberately connecting.

All the conditions are interdependent. Change in any of the three variables—container, differences, or exchanges—results in changes in all of them. Therefore, there is no "finish," but new patterns emerge, behaviors adapt to the new patterns, the patterns shift because of the new behaviors, and so on.

A final consideration on teams using the Core System is self-organized criticality. Over time, moments of change will occur on a team. They may show up as conflicts, breakthroughs, or shifts in coupling, containers, and exchanges. In nature, examples of self-organized criticality include earthquakes, avalanches, forest fires, and other natural events. The size of the change is inversely proportional to the number of changes. In a system with lots of changes, the largest will be massive changes, while a system experiencing fewer changes will have the same proportion of large to small changes, but never massive ones.

Small changes in a system accumulate over time into larger shifts. We can see that happen in a sand pile or in an economic system. The same thing happens on a team. That's one reason we encourage teams to take action and create continually, because the changes that occur from frequent creation will accumulate into larger creative shifts that can then accumulate into massive innovative breakthroughs.

And by using the Core System we can reduce the "white noise" and leave only the music.

Bibliography

Bak, P. *How Nature Works: the Science of Self-organized Criticality*. Oxford: Oxford UP, 1997. Print.

Christakis, Nicholas A., and James H. Fowler. *Connected: the Surprising Power of Our Social Networks and How They Shape Our Lives*. New York: Little, Brown and Co., 2009. Print.

Covey, Stephen R. *The 8th Habit: From Effectiveness to Greatness*. New York: Free, 2005. Print.

Coyle, Daniel. *The Talent Code: Greatness Isn't Born: It's Grown, Here's How*. New York: Bantam, 2009. Print.

Csikszentmihalyi, Mihaly. *Finding Flow the Psychology of Engagement with Everyday Life*. New York: Basic, 2008. Print.

Eoyang, Glenda H. *Coping with Chaos: Seven Simple Tools*. Cheyenne, WY: Lagumo, 1997. Print.

__HSD Professional Certification Training Content, Cohort 15, Ottawa, Canada, Fall, 2010.

___"Conditions For Self-Organizing In Human Systems", The Union Institute and University, 2001

Fisher, Len. *The Perfect Swarm: The Science of Complexity in Everyday Life*. New York: Basic, 2009. Print.

Fried, Jason, and David Heinemeier. Hansson. *Rework*. New York: Crown Business, 2010. Print.

Goldsmith, Marshall, and Mark Reiter. *What Got You Here Won't Get You There: How Successful People Become Even More Successful*. New York: Hyperion, 2007. Print.

McCarthy, Jim, and Michele McCarthy. *Software for Your Head: Core Protocols for Creating and Maintaining Shared Vision*. Boston: Addison-Wesley, 2002. Print.

Meadows, Donella H. *Thinking in Systems*. London: Earthscan, 2009. Print.

Nancy, Kline. *More Time to Think: A Way of Being in the World*. Fisher King, 2010. Print.

Page, Scott E. *The Difference: How the Power of Diversity Creates Better Groups, Firms, Schools, and Societies*. Princeton: Princeton UP, 2007. Print.

Solow, Lawrence, and Brenda Fake. *What Works for GE May Not Work for You: Using Human Systems Dynamics to Build a Culture of Process Improvement*. Boca Raton: CRC, 2010. Print.

Taylor, William. *Practically Radical: Not-so-crazy Ways to Transform Your Company, Shake up Your Industry, and Challenge Yourself*. New York: William Morrow, 2011. Print.

Wheatley, Margaret J. *Leadership and the New Science: Discovering Order in a Chaotic World*. San Francisco: Berrett-Koehler, 1999. Print.

Biography of the Author

Vickie Gray is an international management advisor, certified coach, and McCarthy BootCamp Instructor. A career in IT Service Management consulting, training and coaching that began in 1998, with forays into software development and project management, as well as time spent on volunteer committees and in community projects, have provided an excellent education in the behaviour of human systems.

With her beloved partner, Paul Reeves, she coaches and advises smart individuals and teams on how to create time. They live on a beautiful small farm in Nova Scotia and are owned by two clever greyhounds and a flock of grumpy chickens.

To contact her, email Vickie@simplerulesandtools.com.

Made in the USA
Charleston, SC
26 August 2012